PART II: SLIPPERY SNAKES

Book Two of the Trilogy
More Snakes Than Ladders
(1970 – 1981)

R.D. Craze

Copyright © 2013 R. D. Craze. All rights reserved.

No part of this book may be reproduced or transmitted in any form or by any means, graphic, electronic, or mechanical, including photocopying, recording, taping, or by any information storage retrieval system, without the permission, in writing, of the publisher.

Acknowledgement

Artist—**Lisa Paston**

"I thank again my daughter-in-law Lisa for updating the

cover of this second volume of

More Snakes Than Ladders"

-R. D. Craze

Table of Contents

PROLOGUE

CHAPTER 1........CONTINUED SUCCESS

CHAPTER 2.........HOUSE DISASTERS/HOLIDAYIN SPAIN

CHAPTER 3.........TAKING JAN WITH ME ON BUSINESS

CHAPTER 4........TAKING CARE OF ORDERS/JAN WISHED I WAS A FARMER

CHAPTER 5.........MIKE DRUCE TAKING 3 MONTHS OFF

CHAPTER 6.........A NEW ENTERPRISE

CHAPTER 7........THIS CAN'T BE HAPPENING

CHAPTER 8........TALKS WITH CHARLES SCHOENFELD

CHAPTER 9........ORDERS FROM UNIGULF SERVICE/FOUND MIKE DRUCE'S SECRET HIDING SPACE

CHAPTER 10......HELPING CHARLES SCHOENFELD

CHAPTER 11......FACE TO FACE WITH MIKE DRUCE

CHAPTER 12......I HAD NO IDEA OF THE DANGER I WAS IN

CHAPTER 13......SCHOENFELD VERY ILL & NEEDED MY HELP

CHAPTER 14......TIME OFF FROM WORRIES

CHAPTER 15......AMERICAN HOIST/MIKE JONES AFFAIR

CHAPTER 16......JAN PREGNANT/FRIENDLY NEIGHBOURS

CHAPTER 17......SCHOENFELD DIED

CHAPTER 18......GRASPING AT STRAWS

CHAPTER 19......TAKING FAMILY AWAY

CHAPTER 20......CHAOTIC BUSINESS & HOMELIFE

CHAPTER 21......NEED TO TRY AGAIN

CHAPTER 22......JAN PUT HER FOOT DOWN

CHAPTER 23......GAMBLE DID NOT PAY OFF

CHAPTER 24......DESPERATE TO SURVIVE

CHAPTER 25......MANAGEMENT ON THE MOVE

CHAPTER 26......HOME LIFE CRISIS

CHAPTER 27......JAN COULDN'T PUT UP WITH IT ALL

CHAPTER 28......MY SISTER'S 2ND MARRIAGE/& WALES

CHAPTER 29......SURPRISE BIRTH OF TWINS

CHAPTER 30......A NEW MEANS OF SUPPORT

CHAPTER 31......FAMILY HOLIDAY IN DORSET

CHAPTER 32......INTERIOR DESIGN BUSINESS

CHAPTER 33......CHRISTMAS/JAN WAS OVERWHELMED

CHAPTER 34......A NEW ENTERPRISE

CHAPTER 35......I NEEDED TO COUNT MY BLESSINGS

CHAPTER 36...... THE NARANGS/TOO TRUSTING/

     1975 HOLIDAY

CHAPTER 37......1976/ PROGRESSING/ANOTHER SHOCK

CHAPTER 38......CORNWALL

Prologue :

The Snakes were Rising

I had arrived at the Army and Navy club in Pall Mall to meet a Professor Ronald Stark. I didn't know what to expect from the meeting, I only knew that the demand letters I had sent out had caused an extreme reaction. I had received threatening phone calls in the middle of the night with dire warnings of what might happen to me and my family. They had become so persistent, waking me in the early hours of the morning, anonymous and frightening, so much so that I had ended up pulling the telephone out of the wall, breaking the wire and disconnecting it. Now with this meeting called out of the blue, I didn't know what to expect.

The commissioner showed me through to a large oak paneled room with a high ceiling hung with chandeliers and an oak floor covered with expensive Chinese carpets. There were large Chesterfield armchairs and settees, surrounding a substantial coffee table, along with small individual side tables. There was a large marble fireplace on the far wall, with a flickering welcoming fire and two high backed antique armchairs either side. As I entered, a rotund man in his early fifties with a round face, thick black hair, and a dark swarthy skin, walked over to me. He was shorter than me and had a Mediterranean appearance, exceptionally well dressed, although in a loud striped suit, and as he flashed a smile at me, I saw a glint of gold teeth. He shook my hand and motioned me to the two chairs in the far corner of the room. His friendly demeanor and exaggerated politeness hid a very sinister purpose. He had been sent to see if I should be eliminated...

Chapter 1

Continued Success

As 1970 dawned I seemed to have everything. We had just moved into a wonderful new house, I had a beautiful wife and two lovely children and I was in control of a very successful business booming on all fronts. However, I didn't realise how fragile everything was. In the previous year the only set back had been the loss of the mill venture in Iran, but this had little impact on me as we had more than we could cope with from all the orders that were still flooding in on Alban Feeds. In the first 18 months trading, we were to show a net profit of £128,000, but much of this was being ploughed into the various subsidiaries and associated companies. In addition to this, as I was to discover later, there was a huge leak, through which thousands of pounds were being siphoned off, but in those halcyon days I knew none of that. I seemed to have achieved everything I wanted; but from the meeting two years earlier in San Francisco, a black cloud had slowly been gathering strength until it loomed over everything, ready to engulf and destroy the world we had created.

***

One cold icy day in January, just after a heavy snow fall, I was late for work in the morning and was in a bit of a rush. I was having to use the Vauxhall Victor, which I still hadn't disposed of, as the Vitesse needed a MOT before I could tax it and I hadn't got round to booking it in. Any way try as I might the Victor wouldn't start, I had a meeting at 10 0'clock and the time was ticking on. I decided I would have to take a chance and use the Vitesse. It should be alright as long as I used the back lanes from our bungalow that came out just at the entrance to Dunstable. When I got to the office I would get Anne Fabretti, my secretary, to book the car in for the MOT. But things didn't quite work out that way. The lanes were very narrow; just one car width but there was seldom any traffic there and especially when they were all iced over as they would be that morning. I suppose I was going faster than I should as I was late, when I came face to face with another car. I braked but on the icy lane the car just cruised forward and came to a stop just hitting the other cars bumper. To my utter dismay, it was a police car. The officer got out and said "You were a bit hasty for these roads weren't you; you were blessed lucky you didn't cause a serious accident". He seemed in a bit of a hurry so he told me to take my car documents and driving licence into Dunstable police station that afternoon. He then got back in his car while I backed up all the way down the lane until there was a place for him to pass. As soon as I got to the office I tried to ring round for an MOT and found a garage that would do it that afternoon. However, after I had taken the car in I had a phone call to say it had failed as it needed new brake shoes on the front and a new front number plate where the morning's collision had cracked it. He said he couldn't possible do it for a couple of days and I should take the car in then. I said I would prefer to leave it with him. It was almost a week before I could take my documents into the police station and when I did they had no record of the incident at all. I reckoned that I was very lucky and probably the policeman was going somewhere he shouldn't and couldn't afford to report it.

***

In February we had a visit from Lee Teng-hui from Taiwan. At that time he was a member of Taiwan's Joint Commission on Rural Reconstruction and he was very interested in our companies feed program. He brought me some lovely wooden carvings of Chinese legends which I still have and later he sent me a beautiful set of carved horses. We were doing very good business in Taiwan and he promised co-operation at a government level. He was a very influential figure and was later to become president of Taiwan. Angelos Economides was still providing us with good business from Greece as was Mantovani in Cyprus. In addition we had large orders from Malaysia, India, Sri Lanka, Burma, Thailand, Kenya and Peru and as well as that we were getting a lot of very good enquiries on the general chemical front. Also I had started to speculate on the pharmaceutical and chemical market, buying up cheap stocks and holding them in a bonded warehouse in Hamburg to sell on a rising market. In February I flew to Amsterdam to buy a quantity of Ergotamine Tartrate that was beginning to be used in ant-histamine drugs & some Vitamin E that was being tipped for various usages. Then in March I flew to Antwerp to buy a quantity of Ascorbic Acid that was being widely publicised as an antidote to colds & Flu. While there I also bought some cheap Chlortetracycline Feed Grade, some Salicylic Acid and some Chloramphenicol. The Chlortetracycline we were able to sell immediately to Peru and two months later I sold some of the Ascorbic Acid and all of the Vitamin E to Dr. Soloman, both at a good profit. Later I sold the Salicylic Acid to D. Coury in St. Kitts in the West Indies for almost double what I paid for it.

***

Around that time Derek Parkhouse in our Czech office informed us that Ferroexport were looking to buy some large cranes and did I know of a good source. He suggested that if he got the specification I should deal with it myself as it would be very large business. After a few enquiries I found that the best supplier for the particular cranes required was American Hoist and Derrick Corporation. I made an appointment to see the Director of the London office, Mike Harris, and at the meeting I discovered that they were not doing any business in Eastern Europe but were anxious to make a break through. I got on very well with the Managing Director and signed up an agency agreement for Alban Merchanting Ltd. to supply American Hoist & Derrick cranes and ancillary equipment to Eastern Europe. It was confirmed by post the following day including my 5% commission on any orders received. Armed with this I decided to meet the buyer in Ferroexport and asked Derek to arrange an appointment. He told me that there would be a new man in charge, but that he would be taking up his new position on the 1st July and therefore it would be best to make my appointment after that as the new man would want the credit for the orders and also he would probably want some tangible gratitude. When I told Jan I could see that she was disappointed that I was going off again so soon after our holiday and when we were just settling in to our new house. She didn't want to be left alone on the new estate, especially as no one had seemed very friendly so far. I suggested that she came with me. I told her that I'm sure she would like Prague and my Mum & Dad would look after the children, it would be fun to go together. As Jan didn't like flying we would go by car and I intended to trade the Vitesse in for something more comfortable. I had given Cormac Martin the Victor to use as his company car.

CHAPTER 2

HOUSE DISASTERS/HOLIDAY IN SPAIN

In the meantime I was spending the weekends getting our new house straight. When we moved in, the back and front gardens were just a sea of mud and the driveway was just a thin layer of hardcore. Initially I decided to have a tarmac drive laid, but the day after the tarmac was put down, while it was still soft, the shop decided to deliver our new bedroom furniture. A large pantechnicon lorry pulled up on our drive, sinking right down into the tarmac. When it pulled away I had two very deep ruts all along the drive. So I had to dig the tarmac up. Then my Dad suggested that he help me lay a concrete drive. We would prepare the ground by laying a thick covering of hardcore and get a lorry to deliver readymade concrete which we would tamper down from wooden beam guides on either side. We were quite ambitious with a drive wide enough for two cars side by side in front of the garage and the concrete continuing up alongside the house. Unfortunately the day we chose to lay it was an extremely hot day in May and the ready-mix lorries were the biggest ones available. We were working like maniacs trying to tamp down the concrete before it set hard. By the end of the day we thought we had just achieved it. However in the morning when I awoke I was horrified, the drive looked like a frozen sea and a rough sea at that. It was a constant ripple of solid hard waves. I decided to pull the cars up onto it anyway – I had parked them in the road while the drive was being done. When I came to move my car I couldn't find the car keys anywhere and the bunch not only had the car keys on it but also house keys and the keys to the Dunstable and London offices. I wracked my brains trying to think were they could possibly be and when I had them last. Then to my horror I remembered, they were in the trousers I was wearing to lay the concrete as I had moved the car just before the hardcore arrived. I searched around everywhere outside and then it dawned on me; they must be under the concrete. Jan hated the drive anyway so there was only one thing for it. On Monday I had two men round with pneumatic drills to take the concrete drive up and there, sure enough when the concrete had been removed, was my bunch of keys. After that I decided to get the professionals in and they laid a very nice drive of coloured paving stones and while they were about it I got them to lay a large patio out the back of the same coloured stones. They were a lovely couple of chaps who looked identical to Little & Large, a couple of comedians popular at the time. I did redeem myself however in laying out the garden with a nice curved path from the patio steps and a pretty selection of shrubs and flowers. But my crowning glory was putting up the shed at the end of the garden which I did all on my own, standing on the wooden floor and balancing the roof on my head whilst trying to secure the walls. The neighbours later told us they had never seen such an entertaining cabaret and they were amazed when I finally walked away from it and the shed remained standing. The only other embarrassment was the prize conifer we had brought from the bungalow which we had planted in a prime position in front of the house. It slowly turned brown and died as did the turf lawn we had carefully laid in the front.

***

As mentioned before, my mum and dad often stayed at some holiday apartments in Torremelinos Spain, which at that time was only just making the first tentative steps as a tourist resort away from its regular occupation as a fishing village. The apartments were owned by Cyril Coggins who Mum and Trisha had got friendly with when they went to Spain after Bob, Trisha's husband, died. They were spending a month out there in June 1970 and suggested that Jan & I join them for a couple of weeks as the children were now old enough to travel without too much hassle. So on the 11th June Jan and I with Mark and Troy flew out to Malaga where we were picked up at the airport and taken to Cyril Coggins holiday complex in Torremolinos. I had booked a return flight on BEA and I found out afterwards the flight alone had cost more than a full board all inclusive two week package holiday. As I said earlier Torremolinos was still a small dusty village with only a few holiday hotels and apartments. Ours was very nice with its own pool and play area for the children but most of the other holiday makers seemed to be German. This was particularly noticeable when I went down to the bar to watch the World Cup on the large television there. It was the quarter finals between Germany and England and the bar was filled with Germans. In the second half England were 2-0 up but I didn't feel that I could cheer in that company. Then Germany scored a goal in the 68th minute and they started cheering and thumping the tables and the whole bar erupted when they scored the second goal eight minutes from time. Germany scored again in extra time and won the match – I quietly slunk out of the bar leaving everybody else to party the night away. When the next day we went down to the beach it was practically empty despite the lines of umbrellas and sun loungers. Mark and Troy were happy playing in the sand while Mum and Dad stretched out on the sun loungers. Jan and I went for a walk along the beach, it was beautiful, warm with a gentle breeze and when we paddled in the water it was like a warm bath. The next day Cyril took us all for a drive up into the surrounding hills, stopping at the small villages where he seemed to know people who invited us in for coffee and soft drinks.

***

Mark & Troy loved it in the complex where there were several children their age although they were all Spanish or German, but they seemed to understand each other and with either Mum & Dad or Jan & I supervising them they could go in the paddling pool, drive around in the toy cars or play on the swings and slides in the play area. Once Jan & I decided to go for a walk and we seemed to walk miles along the dusty roads until the heat became unbearable and we longed for shade but we could find none and by the time we wended our way back to the village we were exhausted and dying of thirst. Another day we all went to a beach near

Malaga. We had been told that it was a beach favoured by the locals and we went by bus along the dusty roads. The Spanish love children and they made such a fuss of Mark and Troy and the fuss continued when we got to the beach. A crowd of them insisted that we join them for huge plates of paella being cooked on the beach. When I went to pay they were offended and insisted that we were their guests. Both Jan & I thought it was the best paella we had ever tasted both before and since. All in all it was a lovely holiday and just the break we needed from all the chaos and pressure we had been under. On the return flight the plane was quite empty and the stewardesses made up beds for Mark and Troy on the empty seats and they slept all the way back. When we arrived back in Harpenden there was a postcard from Jenny, Mike Druces ex-secretary who was on holiday in Spain. She asked whether we had been to Torremolinos as she was lying out on a sun lounger when she was sure that as she looked up she had seen someone looking like me walking along by the sea. She knew it must have been someone on holiday by the sun reflecting of the glaring white body.

CHAPTER 3

TAKING JAN WITH ME ON BUSINESS

When we got back I had to set about buying a new car as in a month's time I was taking Jan on her first business trip with me and the Vitesse wouldn't be very comfortable for such a long trip. One evening I had just returned from the London office and was upstairs reading a bedtime story to Mark and Troy when the telephone rang. Jan answered it and called up the stairs that it was our neighbours opposite and they had just rung to see if I could remove my car from their front garden. They weren't particularly happy as they thought it would come through their lounge window, but luckily it had come to rest against their wall. I quickly rushed over and was profuse in my apologies and offered to pay for any damage. As regards the car, it appeared that there was something wrong with the handbrake as it had come away from its anchorage. When I showed them what had happened they were very understanding and told me not to worry, it was just the lawn and flowerbeds damaged. The next morning I took the car to the garage at the bottom for the brake to be repaired and I noticed on the forecourt a relatively new Rover 2000 that the workman had just finished cleaning out. I asked Frank Pratley, the owner if it was for sale and he said it was so after we had agreed a price I bought it. I left the Vitesse with him to be repaired as I intended to sell it later. I now had my nice comfortable car to take Jan to Czechoslovakia.
***
At the end of June Derek Parkhouse informed us that the new man had been installed at Ferroexport and he had made an appointment for me to meet him on 17th July. He had made discreet enquiries and he was susceptible to inducements if discreetly handled. So on the 15th July Jan & I dropped the children off at my mother and fathers house, we expected to be away for about four nights as Jan

didn't like to leave the children for too long. We drove to Harwich and caught the overnight ferry to Bremenhaven. It was a bit off a rough crossing and I felt a bit queasy but Jan took it in her stride. When we arrived in Bremenhaven the weather was foul and as soon as we were on the autobahn the windscreen wipers packed up. With the torrential rain it was difficult to see and I had to keep stopping to clear the windscreen. What with that and having to drive slowly it was a long trip. However as the day wore on the rain cleared and the sun broke through which made driving a little easier except when we got behind a lorry, or a car overtook us splattering the windscreen, when again I had to get out to wipe it clear. We pulled over near Frankfurt for a late lunch and I managed to find a garage to fix the windscreen wipers but it took a great chunk out of the spending money I taken with us. After that the drive to Prague was uneventful and we arrived late at our hotel. Derek had booked us into a new hotel, the International, which was a little way off Wenceslas Square. Apparently there was a large delegation from the Warsaw Pact countries that had taken over the Alcron and the Yalta. I was disappointed as the new hotel, whilst very swish, had none of the atmosphere of the other two. Both Jan and I were exhausted from the long drive so we went straight to bed.

***

The next morning at breakfast we bumped into a colleague from the Czech agency, Terry Richards, who handled sales in the toys and novelties department. After breakfast I left Jan talking to Terry whilst I met with Derek Parkhouse who had come over to the hotel to give me a briefing about Mr. Jaroslav Zdenek, the new buyer at Ferroexport, who I was to meet later. When I rejoined them after Derek had left, Jan told me that Terry had kindly offered to show her round Prague while I had my meeting at Ferroexport which Terry had said she would find boring. It seemed a good idea and I suggested that I join them in the Yalta bar as soon as my meeting finished which I expected to be no later than three o'clock. Jaroslav Zdenek was a very smartly dressed individual in his late thirties and seemed to be less stiff and formal than the usual Czech buyers. I showed him all the brochures and specifications for the cranes he wanted and managed to answer most of his questions. We haggled over the price but I knew my baseline and was pleased when we concluded the deal at £350,000, a little above that. Delivery was required late 1971 and that fitted into the timescale given to me in London. We shook hands on the deal and just as I was about to leave he said that there was another enquiry that I may be interested in. He knew that Machinexport in Hungary were also looking to buy cranes but if I wanted the business I would have to act quickly. If I was interested he could arrange a meeting for me with them in Budapest tomorrow when I could show them all the information I had on American Hoist & Derrick. He would get from them the specification for the cranes I wanted and have the information sent round to my hotel later in the afternoon so that I could get the price structure from my suppliers. I thanked him profusely and said that I would make the arrangements immediately. As I got up to go he put his fingers to his lips and passed me an envelope and then ushered me out. I put the envelope in my pocket and left to meet Terry and Jan at the Yalta Bar. I arrived before them so I took out the envelope and read the letter inside. In it Jaroslav Zdenek stated that certain commissions were payable to an external organisation should my suppliers be granted the order. A bankers' guarantee had to be lodged prior to granting of the order with the Bank of Geneva for the sum of £20,000 payable on delivery of the order and made out to Messrs. Fischler and Webb. Should any further orders be received from any other Warsaw pact country then a similar bankers' guarantee for the same amount was to be lodged for each order. Unless the bank confirmed that such guarantees were in place no orders would be issued. If such conditions were acceptable I was to tell the person delivering the specification for the Hungarian cranes that everything was in order. I needed to telephone Mike Harris of American Hoist and Derrick Corp. in London to ensure that he could go along with the arrangement and to tell him of the Hungarian enquiry. If necessary I would need him to stay on at the office until I could get back to him with the specification so that I could get a quote to take with me the next day. Mike went along with the requirement which I had outlined to him in very oblique terms, in case it was overheard, and said he would wait at the office for as long as it takes.

***

When I returned to the lounge Terry and Jan were there. Jan said that she had a lovely time and that they had been to the Tusek Store on Wenceslas Square and across the Charles Bridge and round the old town. I was happy for her but secretly I wished it had been me showing her around and pointing out all the places that I knew and what they meant to me, but I had planned to do that the following morning. Instead we were going to have to spend the whole day going to Hungary and back. Anyway at least they hadn't been to the Monastery Gardens and that evening I planned to take Jan up there for a meal. First I had to explain how we were off to Budapest in the morning and probably wouldn't get back till late evening. Jan, practical as ever, asked how I could afford it as we didn't have a lot of money left after paying for the windscreen wipers to be fixed. In those days it could take anything up to a week to get money transferred to Eastern Europe and cheques weren't accepted and there were no such things as credit cards. I realised that it was going to be difficult but we had filled the car up with petrol for the return journey and the Rover had two tanks so that would be sufficient. Our hotel had been paid for and so had the ferry. If we had a good breakfast before we left for home and bought a snack for the journey, it wouldn't do us any harm to go one night without a meal if we had to and we would make up for it when we got back. Anyway with the money I had I could afford to take her out that evening and buy a meal the following day in Budapest so she wasn't to worry. Just then my name was announced over the tannoy that I was wanted in reception. It was Zdeneks secretary with the Hungarian

crane specification and the details of our meeting with Machinexport the following day. I told her, as requested that everything was in order and then asked Terry and Jan to excuse me whilst I put in a call to London. I read all the specification out to Mike Harris and he said that he would send me a detailed quote by telex that evening ready for my trip. I gave him the hotel's telex number and then went down to reception and asked them to arrange for two return airline tickets to Budapest for the following day for the earliest flight possible. I also told them that I was expecting a telex that evening but that I would be out and would collect it from reception on my return. I then rejoined Jan & Terry in the lounge and told Jan that it was all fixed and we were off the Budapest in the morning. That evening I took Jan to the Monastery Gardens. It was a hot balmy evening and we had a lovely stroll around the gardens first before going to the restaurant. We were given a table out on the terrace under the arbour overlooking the city below us and as the darkness fell the lights flickered on over Prague and the Charles Bridge lighting up the river, Jan said that she hadn't seen anything so romantic. The meal was good and afterwards the waiter asked us if we would like their new special desert, it was called Sputnik. We both said yes and he came out carrying two plates on a tray with what appeared to be two towers of ice cream with lighted sparklers stuck in the top. Jan and I found it difficult to hide our laughter as they were placed down with great ceremony in front of us. Jan couldn't stop giggling all the time she was eating it.
***

The next day we caught a taxi to the airport and flew to Budapest. It was a bumpy internal flight and Jan hated it. When we arrived in Budapest we had our first problem, we had not arranged any entry visas. We were taken into the guard's office and told that we would not be allowed into the country. I pleaded with them and Jan sat there looking demure and showing her lovely legs in her short mini skirt. That seemed to have more effect than all my entreaties. I noticed that all the time they were talking to me they were looking at her. Then she said in her sweetest voice "Can't you phone the man we are visiting to vouch for us, after all we will be going back as soon as we have seen him". The guards looked at each other and then nodded. I gave them the details of our contact in Machinexport and one of the guards left to make the phone call. When he came back, addressing Jan not me he said "Your husband can have his meeting but you must not rush back from here without seeing something of our beautiful city. We will allow you the day in Budapest but we must have your word that you will leave on the evening flight". Jan opened her big eyes and said how wonderful he was and how eternally grateful we were and that we would not forget his kindness. I was beginning to get a little worried that he might want Jan to show her gratitude in a more tangible way, especially when I saw the way he was looking at her but luckily, after his colleague brought in the paperwork, he just made a little bow to her and waved us out.

***

We went straight to Machinexport and I suggested that Jan came into the meeting with me. I saw how she worked the guards and I thought she might be an asset if Mr. Nagy, the buyer could be similarly entranced. Whether he was or not I don't know but I know that we left the meeting with an order for £750,000 worth of cranes after an hour of intense discussion. With time on our hands Jan & I went for a wander around Budapest. It comprises two distinct parts, the old city of Buda on one side of the river Danube and Pest on the other. We wandered round the narrow streets and steep alleyways of Buda and along the main street where I pointed out to Jan the bullet holes and scars still left from the uprising of 1956. We crossed over an elegant bridge into Pest and along the tree lined boulevards and up Rakocvi Avenue where we found a little café. There we had a lovely meal and coffee before continuing our walk. We then caught a taxi to the airport and our flight back to Prague. Luckily it was less bumpy that the fight out. As we arrived back in our hotel room I had good reason to feel pleased with the trip, I had earned for my company a commission of £55,000, Jan had enjoyed her trip and had seen both Prague and Budapest.

***

The next day after a hearty breakfast we set out for home. We stopped off at Pilsen as I wanted to show Jan the old town and get some orange juice and bread, cheese and ham for lunch. After paying for those I realised that I didn't have a penny left but we shouldn't need any money again until we got home. After we passed through the border into Germany I suggested that Jan should have a drive as it was a comfortable and easy car to drive. She was a little nervous at first but she agreed and she soon relaxed and seemed to be enjoying it. We were cruising along the autobahn when I suddenly noticed the time. I told Jan that we would need to get a move on to make sure that we were in enough time to meet the ferry. I was resting with my eyes closed; when I opened them I was shocked to see that the speedometer was registering 129 mph. I asked Jan to slow down but it was too late, I could already see steam coming out of the bonnet and the temperature gauge was rapidly rising. It was my fault as I had asked Jan to go faster but I didn't think that the car was capable of doing that. We pulled over to the hard shoulder and opened the bonnet. The car was bubbling and steaming and, without thinking I undid the radiator cap, burning my hand. I just dodged in time to avoid the spitting water and burning steam that now enveloped the engine. We sat there waiting for the car to cool down and decided to have our lunch while we waited. We had already drunk the orange juice and my bladder was full. Then I had an idea. I could pee into the orange juice bottle and use that to help fill the radiator. If I could do it twice then there might be enough in it to get us to Bremerhaven before it overheated again. The car seemed to have cooled down a bit so I filled the bottle as discreetly as I could and poured it in quickly and then filled it again. After pouring that lot in, I replaced the radiator cap and waited a little while before starting the engine. Jan said that she didn't want to drive anymore and could I take over. I was getting worried about the time now

as it was getting late and we couldn't afford to miss the ferry, but I was nervous about driving the car too fast in case it overheated again. As it was the engine was still running hot and I had to keep slowing down to keep it from boiling.
***

We got to Bremerhaven just in time too see the ferry leave. The next sailing wouldn't be until the evening after next. Then I remembered that the same line ran a ferry from the Hook of Holland to Harwich on alternate days in the mornings and if we drove through the night we would get there in time and our tickets would be valid for either sailing. After checking the map we set off for the Dutch border. We would need to drive through the night if we were to meet the sailing from the Hook in good time, we had to check in by 8 o'clock in the morning and we needed to drive slow and steady. At about 5.00 a.m. the car started making funny noises. We were miles from anywhere travelling down an empty road. Suddenly there was an almighty bang and the car was covered in clouds of steam or smoke. The engine was dead and all we could do was push the car to the side of the road. Dawn was breaking and we could just make out in the distance a lonely farmhouse. It was too early to go calling, so we decided to try to snatch a few minutes sleep in the car. It was coming up to seven o'clock when we noticed some movement from the farmhouse, it was time to go calling.
***

We got out of the car and walked down the lane to the farmhouse. We didn't really know what we were going to do, we didn't have a penny between us, and all we had was a defunct car that we couldn't even pay to get repaired. Not only that, we were tired and hungry and dishevelled, from our night in the car, and it was an ungodly hour to go calling on people. Full of trepidation I knocked on the door. It was opened by a thin angular woman in her sixties who looked very surprised to see us. I asked if she spoke English and when she said she did, Jan apologetically told her our story. To our relief her face broke into a smile, and she invited us in, insisting that we join her and her family for breakfast, while we all decided what could be done. We were shown into a huge farmhouse kitchen with a large table in the centre. There was a younger woman in there with a child of about seven, and the woman introduced them as her daughter-in-law and her grandchild. She said that her husband and son were out on the farm and would be back shortly. Then she started talking to her daughter-in-law in Dutch and seemed to be explaining our situation while Jan sat talking to the little girl, who apparently could understand what she was saying. A few minutes later the woman's husband and son came in, and we were introduced. Again the woman launched into her monologue, explaining our position. There were smiles and handshaking all around, and then the he husband shook his head with gravity, saying "it's bad for you, we must see what can be done, but first breakfast". Two extra chairs were brought in and we all sat round the table. He had a nobly, ruddy round face, wispy grey hair, and a slightly portly build, while his son was dark haired, thin and muscular with black framed glasses. His wife was a little plain with mousey brown hair and a thin sparse figure, but she had a lovely smile. Their daughter was a pretty little blonde girl, who seemed to take to Jan, and they giggled together, but what about I don't know. Breakfast was a cold collage of almost every sort of cold meat, a bowl of tomatoes, various pickles and a rustic loaf of bread. The farmer pointed to one of the meats and said that it was horse, and did we mind. He had heard that the English were funny about that. Both Jan & I said that we didn't mind at all, and that we were very grateful for their kindness. The woman then piled our plates with all the different meats saying that she wanted to make sure that we ate well, as we might have a long wait before we could eat again. Jan and I tucked in to the meat, tomatoes, bread and homemade pickles – it all tasted delicious, and then it was all washed down with several cups of coffee. They were all so nice and friendly, except the son who sat quietly not saying much. After breakfast we sat around talking a little, and

then we were asked how we were to get home. I said that our only chance was to catch the next ferry from Bremerhaven, which sailed the following evening, but that we would have to leave our car and go back for it at another time. The mother then said that her son would run us back to Bremerhaven, and he would give us the money for a hotel. We could reimburse him when we got back to England. The farmer said we could tow the car into his field next to the house, for the time being. Jan had been chatting to the mother, who offered to let us wash and freshen up before leaving. Soon we were cleaned up, with a change of clothes and ready to hit the road. I kept looking at the son, he had said nothing, and didn't seem over happy about the situation, but he was bundled along by his mother and father, even his wife seemed quite sweet about it. We kept repeating how grateful we were, and how kind they had been. We recognized how inconvenient it was going to be for their son to have to take us all that way, and then return, but his father said he had business in Hamburg that he could see to, and it was no trouble. We couldn't thank them enough, and told them we could never repay their kindness, but as soon as we got back to England would be sending them a check. They insisted that it was the least they could do, and no trouble at all. We were certainly unbelievably lucky! How extraordinary, to have knocked on the door of such good people. What we would have done otherwise, is not something I like to contemplate. However, throughout all this, the son remained taciturn. By the time we were all ready to leave it was almost 1.00 p.m. and it was a good few hour's drive to Bremerhaven, so we would be lucky to get there by early evening.
***

Once in the car, and on our way, the son put on the car radio very loud, and didn't speak a word until we arrived in Bremenhaven. He then pulled up outside a sleazy seaman's hotel and went inside. He came back and told us that he had paid them for a room for us for the night. He then got our cases out of the boot and dumped them on the pavement. With no more ceremony he got back into his car and drove off, leaving us standing on the pavement with our cases. It was about six thirty in the evening and we were stranded with no money in what appeared to be a very rough part of Bremenhaven. We don't believe this is what the farmer and his wife had in mind for us, and obviously their son had some resentment towards us, especially when he was roped into driving us to the ferry, perhaps this was payback time! But that was okay, we knew how incredibly lucky we had been so far.

***

We didn't know how far we were from the ferry point, or how we were going to get there in the morning. We decided that all we could do was to check into our room, and ask where we had to go to catch the ferry. The room was dirty and depressing but we felt exhausted – we had virtually no sleep the night before, so we decided to go straight to bed and sort everything out in the morning. We had a quick wash in the bathroom down the landing, and then collapsed into bed. Apart from one incident in the night when we were woken by loud noises of arguing in the street outside, and we both needed to use the toilet down the corridor, (despite Jan being frightened to leave the room, we made it there and back without incident), we slept soundly until the morning, until about 8.30 a.m. in the daylight, the bathroom looked even grimier than the night before, and there was no shower. We dressed and went down to the reception, and not to our surprise, found no breakfast was included in the price. Well, we would just have an early start. At reception, they told us that the ferry sailing to Harwich, was at 5.30 p.m. but that we should report there at least an hour beforehand if possible. It was about two miles to the ferry port and we had no money for food or bus fares, let alone a taxi, so we would have to walk with our cases, but at least we wouldn't have to hurry. We were given directions and made a slow meander through the streets arriving at the port at about 12.30 p.m. We checked in our luggage and were told that we would probably be able to board the ferry at 4.00 p.m. so we had three and a half hours to kill. We decided to take a wander round the docks but first I had to make a transfer charge call to my office to make sure that someone would be there to collect us at Harwich when we arrived the next morning. I also realised that, although our tickets gave us a cabin, there was no food included. Both Jan and I already felt hungry, but without any money we would be unable to get anything to eat until we were collected at about 8.30 a.m. the following morning. In my call to the office, I asked them to make sure that whoever came to pick us up, they needed to bring us sandwiches to eat, as soon as we got into the car! We made our way to our cabin and to our relief there was tea making facilities and two biscuits each. Once we had eaten the biscuits and drunk all the tea, we both had a shower and cuddled up in bed, hoping to sleep the hours away, but hunger made us have a fitful sleep, We awoke early, and started to get ready. The boat docked at 7.00 a.m. and we made sure we were one of the first off. After hanging about to collect our luggage, and then go through customs, we made our way to the exit. There to our immense relief, was Cormac Martin, with two bacon sandwiches, two huge sausage rolls and a flask of tea. We ate the sausage rolls on the way to the car and then once in the car, drank the tea and finished off the bacon rolls. At last we could get back to normality, although we were riddled with indigestion on the way home.

***

Jan declared that would be the first and last business trip she will ever make with me!

Immediately I got to the office, I arranged for a large cheque to be sent to our Dutch benefactors. As for the car, we never did go back to collect it.

CHAPTER 4

TAKING CARE OF ORDERS/JAN WISHED I WAS A FARMER

The following week I went into the office in Jan's car. She had been having trouble with it as the engine would keep cutting out at the most inconvenient times. The last time she had been stranded in the middle of Harpenden High Street and she had felt so embarrassed that she refused to drive the car again until it was fixed. It was an awkward problem to diagnose as it was an intermittent fault. Anyway at lunchtime I dropped the car over to a garage in Luton as it needed an MOT as well and got a lift back to the office, arranging to collect it in the evening.

***

Back at work I put the wheels in motion for the order of cranes for American Hoist & Derrick and ensuring that they gave the necessary instructions to the Swiss Bank for the external commissions, which for the two orders would be £40,000 for Mr. Zdenek. The order would take twelve months to deliver before I could get my commission which would be a very healthy £55,000. Then I left early to collect Jan's car and I was driving it back to Harpenden when suddenly the bonnet flew up and snapped off, going completely over the top of the car and landing up in the road behind. Luckily there was no car immediately following me. Someone at the garage hadn't fastened the bonnet down. I collected the now battered bonnet and put it on the verge. Then I drove back to the garage minus the bonnet with the car looking like a hot-rod. I explained to the garage what had happened and they tried to say it wasn't their fault but considering I had only just left them and hadn't stopped anywhere else they had to concede that it might have not have been secured by them. However without admitting formal liability they agreed to replace the bonnet if I would leave the car with them. They then run me home, collecting the old battered bonnet on the way. When I got in and told Jan she just said "Why do these things always happen to you."

***

As we suspected other feedstuff companies were starting to copy our ideas and our most aggressive competitor was Coburn Vitafeeds Ltd. They were undercutting our prices to try to get into our markets and with some success. Being the first in the field we still had the largest share of the business with several loyal customers but it wouldn't be long before things started to even out and we did not have the multi-million pound backing to undertake a price war against the likes of BOCM and Coburn. However with our set-up at least Nick Nicholls with Guinness Chemical Co. could cash in on our rivals success as they were still supplying them with the majority of raw materials required in the supplements. In addition our diversification should allow us over time to compensate for the decrease in the feedstuff business. Also in October I took Jan and the boys down to Devon to stay for a few days at John Donnithornes farm in Cullompton. John & I had remained in touch after he left the Czech agency and he had bought a livestock farm down there. He was very happy as a farmer and I had supplied him with some veterinary medicines at trade prices and did all his printing for him through Alban Press. Now I had sold him my sister's late husband's shotgun and I took the opportunity of the break to deliver it to him. I had met his wife many years ago when both John & I worked together. I was a keen history buff and I liked Shakespeare and there had been a season of Shakespearian histories on television and John had invited me to dinner each week at his house in Blackheath when they were on, to explain to him the historical background. His wife was a lovely woman and an excellent cook. She was also a direct descendant of the Plantagenet kings of England, but she was very down to earth and I knew that Jan would like her. They had one child, a boy, whom they nicknamed Toad.

Apparently when he was a baby John was holding him above his head when the baby pooped all over him. John exclaimed "You dirty little toad" and the name had stuck. We had a lovely holiday and John showed Jan and the boys the little calves and pigs and how to milk the cows. As we drove back Jan said that she wished I was a farmer as that was the life she really wanted.

CHAPTER 5

MIKE DRUCE TAKING 3 MONTHS OFF

At the beginning of November I had a phone call from Mike Druce. He said that he had received an order for 15kg of Ergotamine Tartrate, a huge quantity, from a company in Switzerland called Inland Alkaloids. The price of Ergotamine had been climbing steadily but of late it seemed to have bottomed out. We had a stock of 5kgs in Hamburg which I had bought cheap earlier that year and we would need to buy the rest. Mike said that he had agreed a selling price of £3.15s. per gram but I knew the best price I could buy the 10kgs at would be £3.8s. per gram, although I had bought the 5kgs earlier at £2.5s. per gram. The overall deal would give us a nice healthy profit of £11,000. I suggested that we split the order in two and sell 5kgs immediately from stock and back to back the other 10 kilos which we had to buy in, but Mike said that we were cash rich at the moment and we should buy the 10kilos straight away in case the price increased. He would square it with the bank for any excess cash we might need, but that would only be necessary if we made any other large purchases in the meantime. That seemed fair enough so I purchased the 10kilos for delivery to our warehouse in Hamburg. At the beginning of December, with all the material in stock I issued drafts and a collection order through our bank to be released on payment of £56,250. As soon as payment was received against the drafts the bank had an irrevocable instruction to release the collection order, which upon presentation at the warehouse would enable the consignment to be collected. It followed our usual pattern of selling ex stock and saved us the process and charges for delivery, although it was more usual when selling between agents and brokers in the Hamburg and Amsterdam markets.

***

At our Christmas get together the following week Mike Druce surprised us by announcing that he was going on a three month holiday to Egypt and the Middle East immediately after Christmas. He hoped to do some business during the second half of his holiday but he was suffering from exhaustion and the doctor had recommended he took a break as he had been overdoing it. Also he owed it to his wife as she had been having a bit of a rough time. He had managed to get a good deal through his sister who was working with a travel agency. He said that Charles Druce business was a bit slack at the moment and the secretary could take care of the routine stuff and perhaps I could keep an eye on it for him. It seemed to us that he was perhaps overdoing the break a bit by taking so long and he had never seemed to show much concern for his wife before but maybe he was turning over a new leaf. Although Nick Nicholls, forthright as ever, said if anyone had been overworking it was Ronnie but he never disappeared for months on end and come to that we could all do with a break adding that some of us were obviously more dedicated than others. All of which seemed to go over Mike Druce's head as he ignored it. Instead he said that he would be leaving for home now, he would be around for a week and then he would give us details of where he could be contacted in an emergency. With that he was gone.

CHAPTER 6

A NEW ENTERPRISE

Just before Christmas the Harpenden Rotary Club used to tour round the estate with Father Christmas sitting in a makeshift sledge on the back of a truck accompanied by his helpers in their elf suits giving out sweets to the any children or youngsters. It was our first Christmas in our new house and Mark and Troy were very excited as we waited in the road at the bottom of our drive. We could hear the music some distance away when Troy suddenly said that he needed to go to the toilet. I went back and let him in the house and then returned to wait with Jan and Mark by the road. Soon the cavalcade was almost ready to turn down into our road and there was still no sign of Troy. I rushed back to hurry him up as he was in danger of missing everything. I expected him to be in the downstairs toilet but he was upstairs in the bathroom and he had locked himself in. I knocked on the door and asked him to open it but he couldn't as the lock was stuck. He was just a little over two and a half years old and I don't know why he had locked the door, we never had before. It was no good, try as we might there was no way of opening it and Troy couldn't move it from his side. I went outside, the cavalcade had past and people were making their way back. It was about six o'clock and I could see a light on in one of the half finished houses at the bottom of the cul-de-sac opposite. I asked Jan to go upstairs and keep Troy happy while I went to see if I could find one of the builders. Luckily one of the carpenters, who had worked on our house, was working late and I explained to him what had happened. Anyway when he came across with me he said that the only way was either to break the door down or take the window frame out. He decided to take the window frame out as he could always put that back but he had no replacement doors. So with his ladder, he took a window out, climbed in and let Troy out. When I asked him what I owed him he said that I was to forget about it as it was Christmas and the little boy had already missed out on his Christmas treat. For a while after that he would often drop by the house on his way back and come in for a cup of tea and a chat. Jan and I thought that he was probably lonely and we nicknamed him Dobbin as he was like some old faithful conscientious workhorse. When the houses were finally finished the workforce moved on and we never saw him again. About this time we acquired a cat. Mark and Troy found it on a building sight and brought it home. They christened it 'Tibby' but really it was a wild feral cat and never became house trained. It would constantly spray Jan's house plants and when we took it to the vets to be neutered he told us that he had never seen so many fleas on a cat before. As well as neutering him he also dealt with his fleas and we bought a flea collar and had the house fumigated, but he was never really domesticated. Later we acquired a little kitten that Jan took pity on in St. Albans market. It was a little black and white fluffy one and we called him Toby. The two cats got on well and we would watch them playing together in the shrubbery in the garden, although Tibby would still disappear for days

***

Jan's mum, dad and brother were spending Christmas day with us. I would forget about business for a week and concentrate on us all having a happy time – and so it was. After the collapse of Peacock Arts I had kept some beautiful soft Welsh leather skins dyed black. They had followed us from Westbury to Harpenden and Jan's mum had offered to make me a leather coat out of them and so on Christmas Day she presented me with a beautiful hand tooled leather coat. I was thrilled. Mark and Troy were inundated with presents from the family and relatives and a few were kept back for Granddad Salmon to give out after dinner when he disappeared and returned dressed as Father Christmas, handing out the remaining presents while we gathered round the Christmas Tree. Mark kept asking where Granddad had gone as he was missing Father Christmas. On Boxing Day we all went for a walk and then my Mum and Dad came over for dinner in the evening. On New Years Eve we went over to my Mum & Dads and there we met Janet Gawn a friend of my sisters' who was visiting with my parents. She said that she had heard that I was always looking for business opportunities and her boyfriend, Don Finlay, had a contact in Abu Dhabi in the Gulf that he sold fibre glass boats to. Apparently this agent was also looking for someone to supply furnishings for a hotel that was being built out there. If I was interested she would give me the address and she gave me the details of Unigulf Services.

CHAPTER 7

THIS CAN'T BE HAPPENING

It was on a Monday the first week of January that I arrived in the office at Dunstable to go through the post. There were several letters among them that Jenny had forwarded from the London office, an arrangement I had made while Mike Druce was away. The first letter I opened from this pile was a letter from the bank informing us that Alban Feeds account was £30,000 overdrawn and that this was an unauthorised overdraft and should be repaid immediately. In the meantime our account was stopped. My first reaction was that the bank had made a mistake as we should be in credit by approximately that amount after the payment from Inland Alkaloids, so I phoned them immediately. I spoke to the Manager's secretary and she confirmed that it was correct; we were £30,000 in the red. I asked her if she could confirm that we had received payment for the Ergotamine Tartrate and after disappearing for a short while she came back to say that no payment had been received and they still had the documents there to be collected. Things didn't seem quite so bad then as, even if they didn't pay up, we still had Ergotamine Tartrate worth at least £45,000 to £50,000 for a quick sale. I decided to send them an ultimatum that, unless we received payment within the next five days we would have to sell the material elsewhere. It would just mean that we couldn't issue any cheques for a week. I assured the secretary that money would be received into the account within the next ten days to eliminate the overdraft.

***

A week elapsed and still there was no reply from Inland Alkaloids, so the first thing was to dispose of at least some of the Ergotamine Tartrate quickly elsewhere. It was still a good market and we should have no problem in selling it off in small parcels. First I needed to notify the warehouse of our intentions and to see how the material was packed. I put a call into the store man to explain to him but I couldn't believe his answer. He said that someone came to the warehouse with a collection order three weeks ago and took the whole consignment. He assumed they must have been Inland Alkaloids as all the documentation was correct. I said that it couldn't have been as the documents were still with the bank, but he was adamant. He had personally checked everything himself and the papers and collection documents were signed by Mr. Druce. I was devastated – it didn't make sense. I checked the order we had from Inland Alkaloids for an address but it was only a post box number in Zurich. I made enquiries through the Swiss Chamber of Commerce but they had no record of such a company. It looked like we had been swindled and what was worse it would seem that Mike Druce was at the centre of it. He had introduced the order from Inland Alkaloids and it looked like he had signed the duplicate papers used to make the collection from our warehouse and now he was somewhere in Egypt. I had to try to get his address so that I could speak urgently to him. There was another thing I couldn't understand. Even without the money for the Ergotamine Tartrate we should still have a few thousand in the bank, in fact Mike Druce himself said that we had more than enough to buy the additional Ergotamine we needed and we had had no major expense since.

***

I asked Mike Jones if he could try to locate Mike Druce while I shot up to the London office to look at the accounts books. Jenny was really helpful, she told me that all the books were in a small safe in Mike Druce's office and she knew the combination as Mike had phoned her once for some information he needed and she had kept a note of the number in case of emergencies. I got all the books out and started going through them. The first thing I noticed was that there seemed to be continual cash transfers from Alban Feeds bank account to Charles Druce Bank account. I totalled the transfers up to about £36,000 which immediately accounted for why the Alban Feeds account was so overdrawn. I needed to see what money was in Charles Druce account to see what we could transfer back to Alban to set against the overdraft, but when I checked Charles Druce bank statements they showed that the account was £3,500 overdrawn. I couldn't find any account books for Charles Druce but I could see from the invoices issued that very little sales had been done in the last few months. I asked Jenny if there were any large sums of money owed to Charles Druce on any transactions and also did she know anything of Inland Alkaloids but she knew nothing of that company as she had never heard of them and as far as she knew there was no outstanding money due in from anything she had dealt with. Just then Mike Jones called. He said that he had drawn a complete blank in trying to locate Mike Druce. He had even phoned Druce's sister but she professed to have no idea where he was staying. I knew the answer before I asked the question but I asked Jenny if she had any way of contacting him but she said that Mike had told her that he would ring through to give her an address and phone number. Needless to say she had received nothing and no contact from him since he left, and she was worried as the landlord had phoned that morning to say that his final demand for rent had been ignored.

***

Things were now looking very serious. We had a frozen bank account, our stocks of Ergotamine had gone and the bank were pressurising us to pay back £30,000. In addition to this we had wages and various bills to meet as well as our normal business expenses to keep trade going and now Druce hadn't even paid the rent on the London office. All we had was a small stock of Vitamin C and Chloramphenicol in Hamburg which I would have to sell immediately, at a loss if necessary and I would have to make sure that it was paid into an account that would stop it being snatched by the bank to set against the £30,000 overdraft. Even that would only keep us going for about another month and it was going to be difficult to buy materials to fulfil orders. I took Jenny into my confidence and told her the situation. I explained I was devastated but I would have to close the London office with immediate effect. After all the time she had been with us I was so sorry but I could only pay her for a couple of months and I would do what I could to help her find another job or, if I could turn things around she was welcome to come back and work for us. In the meantime she could help us out in the Dunstable office. She said that for some time now, ever since her holiday, she had wanted to move to Spain and it was only her loyalty to me that had stopped her. She needed to find a job over there and she didn't mind what she did. I said that I'm sure I could help her with that and I would get my parents to speak to Cyril Coggins to see if he knew of anything. It would take until April to sort things out for her but eventually through his connections she was offered a job as a housekeeper in Benyamina just outside Torremolinos, just temporary at first but it was to turn into a permanent job for her. She gave me her address in Spain in case I could meet her there. We met up when she came back for a week or so in June and then when she returned in September she very kindly offered to help look after the London office when I went on holiday as my sister wasn't available but after that she went back to Spain. As things became increasingly more hectic for me I'm ashamed to say I didn't respond to her letters or forgot to return her call when she tried to phone me so unsurprisingly we lost contact and I never saw her again.

***

Meanwhile Charles Schoenfeld still had the offices below Charles Druce and I thought that possibly he could buy the Chloramphenicol and the Vitamin C immediately at a reduced price and I could ask him to pay the money into some other account. Things had never been particularly cordial with us since I had left him but we had done business together and I had always tried to treat him fairly. Perhaps I could throw myself on his mercy or at least explore the possibility of his help. It was coming up to lunch time and I decided to go down and ask him if I could take him to lunch as there was something I wished to discuss with him. As I entered his offices I asked Jackie, his secretary what sort of a mood he was in. She that he had not been well and was feeling his age but she didn't know what sort of reception he would give me as one minute he was shouting and getting cross and the next he was mellow and thoughtful. I could only risk it, so I went through and asked how he was feeling and that I was pleased to see him. Luckily he was in his mellow mood. He said that he wasn't well and was finding the business too much to manage, he was thinking of giving it all up. I asked him if I could take him to lunch and said we would talk about it there. I asked Jackie to phone through for a table at his favourite fish restaurant, the Hook, Line and Sinker in Baker Street, and then to order a cab. Over lunch Charles told me all his troubles which were mainly medical and how he didn't know how long he could go on. Then he started berating me for leaving him and said that he could really do with my help now. I felt sorry for him and said that perhaps I could help him out if he wanted. I couldn't work full time for him at present but I could certainly spare a couple of days a week and later when my own business affairs were more settled perhaps I could spend longer. In the meantime I told him of what I had discovered about Mike Druce and that I was closing Druce's office. I didn't tell him of the full extent of my financial difficulties as I knew a wily old fox like Schoenfeld would screw whatever advantage he could from it despite my genuine desire to help him, but I did ask him to buy the Ascorbic Acid and Chloramphenicol. We haggled over price and finally struck a deal on the Ascorbic Acid at quite a good price, but what he was offering for the Chloramphenicol I was only prepared to let a quarter of our stock go and then only because I needed as much money as I could quickly. I then told him I needed to open a new account for Alban Merchanting Ltd. away from our other business and could I use his introduction to open an account at his branch of Barclays Bank at Swiss Cottage so that I could fast track it through. He agreed and said that he would make the necessary phone call when he got back to the office and if it was possible we could go to the bank on his way home. Everything seemed to be getting sorted although sitting opposite Charles Schoenfeld in a fish restaurant was a high price to pay. He would eat the whole fish, head and tail, and talk to me with bits of fish hanging out his mouth and every now and again showering me with half masticated fish as he talked. His conversation was continually punctuated with loud grunts, snorts and burps.

***

Back at the office he phoned for the appointment whilst I went back upstairs to ask Jenny to find the Memorandum and Articles of Association and Incorporation Certificate for Alban Merchanting that I knew Mike Druce had somewhere as he dealt with the formation of all the companies. I phoned Mike Jones and told him what I had done and he seemed relieved that we had averted imminent disaster. Charles had managed to make the appointment so I went and collected my car and armed with the documents we went to the bank. Opening the account was a formality and as director and secretary I could fill out most of the documents and I just needed to get Mike Jones' signature as co-director. The manager said that he could let me have a temporary cheque book at the end of the week and Charles Schoenfeld agreed to transfer the money into the new account as soon as we could arrange the transfer of the proceeds of sale. Both the Choramphenicol and the Ascorbic Acid would remain in the warehouse for the time being but I would provide Schonco with a transfer of ownership. At least we could have money for the next few weeks but we needed more business if we were to solve the problem of how we were going to carry on. I took Charles back to his flat and drove back home, I would forget about everything until tomorrow morning. I didn't say anything to Jan as I didn't want her worrying.

***

The next day I phoned to hire a lorry to clear out the offices and arranged to collect it the following Monday. I wanted to make sure that the new account was open and Charles Schoenfeld had paid the money across. Then I phoned Jenny to ask if she could hang on in the London office until the end of the week, after that she could help us out in Dunstable for a few weeks and in the meantime she could man the office as normal. Mike Jones had suggested that we could store everything at the place he and his wife were renting at Eaton Bray. It was an old rectory out in the countryside with a range of outside barns which would do perfectly. I had brought the accounts books and bank stuff back with me to show Mike Jones and I suggested that he look after them for the time being. I then brought Cormac Martin in and explained what had happened. Again I didn't make too much of the financial problems as I didn't want him panicking or telling the girls until I had sorted out how we were to survive. Cormac said that he knew where he could get some tea chests and cardboard boxes so we agreed that Cormac would collect the lorry on Sunday and the chests and boxes keeping them in the lorry overnight. He would then pick me up at about 5 a.m. on Monday so that we could have a full day and miss the morning rush hour. Mike Jones would make his own way up and then we would spend the day packing everything up and totally clearing all the offices and the stocks in the basement. I would go through the papers as we were packing them away to see if I could find any reference to Inland Alkaloids as it was essential that we track them down as quickly as possible. Once the lorry was loaded Mike Jones and Cormac would go back in Mike's car to get everything ready for storage and I would drive the lorry back. Having made all the arrangements I then dictated a letter to Unigulf Services. I had forgotten about them in all the confusion and I didn't really hold out much hope.

***

Monday morning I was up and ready before five as I didn't want Jan to be woken up as I knew how difficult it would be for her to get back to sleep again and there was nothing worse than trying to look after the children when you are tired and worn out. I had explained to Jan that we were closing the London office because we wanted to economise and it was a waste of time having two offices. I explained that Schoenfeld had said that I could use his office when in London. At five o'clock I went outside to wait for Cormac. I was just standing in the drive when I heard my telephone ring back in the house. I rushed back as I was worried that it would wake everyone up, but I was too late. Mark & Troy were on the landing half asleep and Jan was trying to get them back into bed. All my efforts at creeping around trying not to create any disturbance was undone and when I answered the phone it was just Cormac telling me he was on his way. I went up to apologise to Jan but the damage was done, I could hear the boys romping around in the bedroom – wide awake and ready for mischief and I knew that there would be no more rest for Jan. It was going to be a long day.

***

By the time we got to the office it was about 7.30 a.m. and Mike Jones was already there waiting. We unloaded the boxes and tea chests and then Cormac went off to park the lorry. The rest of the day was spent in sorting out papers and files, packing everything up, stacking all the laboratory chemical bottles in the tea chests and dismantling furniture. With an early break for brunch, by four o'clock we were ready to bring the lorry round to start loading. I had not found anything concerning Inland Alkaloids. After all the furniture and boxes were stacked in the lorry Cormac suggested that we should take the carpets as well, after all they were ours. We had just taken up the carpet in Mike Druce's office when I noticed some cut floor boards loose in the corner behind where Mike Druce's desk had been. They constituted a rectangle of about 12ins. by 8ins. that formed a mini trap-door. I lifted them up and underneath I found a small black address book and about twenty little vials of colourless liquid packed in straw in a metal box, also a written synopsis from Lester Friedman of the University of San Diego explaining how it had been discovered that LSD could be synthesised from Ergotamine. As for the vials, I was pretty sure that they contained LSD, whether from Ergotamine synthesis or Lysergic Acid it was impossible to tell although the paper from Friedman would suggest the former. The black address book contained many names and addresses but no clue as to what their significance was. I showed my find to Cormac and Mike Jones. Cormac was all for selling the LSD and getting some money back whereas Mike Jones said that we were in enough trouble already and that we should hand it over to the police. The main trouble with Cormac's proposal was that, although we had our suspicions of what it was, we had no definite proof and it could even be a lethal substance. Besides I didn't really want to get mixed up in that market and if we were wrong or even if we were right and it was contaminated the retribution would be too horrendous to contemplate. So even though we might be looking at a fortune I agreed with Mike Jones that we should hand it over to the police, but I would hang on to the little black book as I was sure that somewhere in its pages lay the people behind Inland Alkaloids.

***

By 6.30 p.m. we were all loaded and ready to go. Mike and Cormac went off in the car and I drove the lorry, slowly at first while I manoeuvred round the traffic as I never driven anything as big before, but once we were out onto the motorway I could settle back and relax. The drive from Dunstable to Mike Jone's house was through a string of winding lanes and by the time I got to that section it was after 8 p.m. and a pitch dark night. The lorry virtually took up the width of the lanes but luckily the odd traffic I met all backed up for me. Then suddenly all my lights went out and I was in pitch darkness. At first I couldn't see a thing but eventually I could make out the dim outline of the bushes on either side. I didn't know what to do. I couldn't leave the lorry where it was as it completely blocked the lane. There was no way I could see anywhere to pull in as I could only make out dim shapes. I knew that the lane I was in finished in a tee-junction and I needed to turn left at that and then take a right turn about a mile further on and I would be in the lane leading to Mike Jone's house which was before you reached Eaton Bray village. I could just make out the lights of that village on the skyline to the left. I had no choice I would have to go on. Very slowly I crept along the lane following the vague shadow of the bushes on either side. After what seemed like an eternity I seemed to drive into something straight ahead. I had reached the tee-junction and in the darkness gone straight into the hedge on the other side. I backed the lorry up and almost felt my way round into the road. Now I had about a mile to go before I needed to turn right but I had no panel lights to see the milometer. The road was a little wider so I followed the hedge line on the left but the wider road meant that I couldn't properly make out the hedge on the right so I couldn't see any break that would denote my turning. I would have to guess when I thought a mile would be up. A short while later a car came the other way and through its shining lights I thought I saw a gap in the hedge row. He flashed his lights furiously as he approached and I was worried that he might not have room to pass but he seemed to squeeze through. After I had reached where I thought I had seen the opening I pulled up and got out to investigate. To my disappointment it turned out to be a farm gate leading to a field. I decided to leave the lorry and walk further up the lane to see if I could find the turning. After about 500yards I found it and I looked round to see if there was anyway I could mark it in the dark. Turning back I noticed a tree on the left hand side which I estimated was about six lorry lengths from the turning so I ran back to the lorry and started it up, then gingerly made my way along looking out for that special tree whose shape I had separated from the others. Eventually I found it; then at some risk I drove over to the right hand side of the road and edged along until I came to the lane opening. I turned into it and again followed the hedge line. Either my eyes were getting more used to the dark or it was slightly lighter along this lane as I could make out the hedges quite distinctly. Then to my immense relief I could see the lights of a large house ahead on my right and a yard light illuminating the barns – I had finally made it. As I turned into Mike's drive I heard Cormac yell out "What on earth kept you so long, we've been here ages and why have you turned your lights off". I jumped from the cab, my head was spinning with the concentration and I told them what had happened. They couldn't understand how I had made it through the lanes. We quickly unloaded the lorry and stored the stuff in the barns. The original idea had been for Cormac to stay the night with Mike and for me to drive the lorry and park it at my place until the morning, but the lorry would have to stay there until morning. Mike said I could stay the night but I said if at all possible I would like to go home if he wouldn't mind giving me a lift. Mike run me home and dropped me outside and said that he would shoot straight back as his wife had dinner ready for him and Cormac. I was also ready for my dinner which I knew Jan would have in the oven for me and I could see by the lights that she had gone to bed after her long day.

***

CHAPTER 9

ORDERS FROM UNIGULF/FOUND MIKE DRUCE'S SECRET HIDING PLACE

After a few days back in the office I received a reply from Unigulf Services with a shopping list of furnishings and items they required for the hotel that was now nearing completion. I spent the next few days phoning around for prices and brochures and the most competitive was from a company called Meredew. So I sent everything off with very little hope of business as this sort of trade was very new to me. Then by the end of the week I had made a decision about the things I had found under Druce's office floor. I would write to all the names in the black book asking them if they had anything to do with a company called Inland Alkaloids. If they did they must pay for the Ergotamine Tartrate they had taken or return it to the store, otherwise I was going to hand the whole matter over to the police. On the Monday, a week after we had cleared Druce's Office, I dictated a letter to all the names in the black book asking whether they had any knowledge of a firm called Inland Alkaloids or the whereabouts of 15kgs of Ergotamine Tartrate that had been illegally collected from our warehouse in Hamburg. I stated that we should receive payment in full for the material or it must be returned forthwith. Unless either of these things happened we would be reporting the matter to the police as it involved both fraud and theft and the nature of the missing material had other more severe implications. As soon as the letters had been done I took them to the Post Office and then went on to the Police Station to hand in the vials of colourless liquid that we had found in Druces office. I explained the situation, that is that I found them in an office I had been to clear out and the owner was abroad, but I wasn't sure what the material was and I didn't want it left hanging around. They got me to sign a statement to that effect and I never heard about it again.

***

A couple of weeks later Jan and I were disturbed by a knock at the door at about 9.30 p.m. When I opened it I was shocked to find Geoffrey, our bank manager from Crystal Palace, on the doorstep. He asked if he could come in as he had an important matter to discuss concerning the overdraft at Alban Feeds Ltd. I invited him in and offered him a cup of tea - I was still very surprised to see him at that time of night as he had obviously travelled over from the other side of London. Anyway he said that he knew that freezing our account would have a debilitating affect on the company and that we would find it impossible to trade, which was a shame as we appeared to have a very healthy business. The problem was that he could not allow the overdraft to continue unsecured and unless we were prepared to guarantee it the bank would be forced to call in the loan and if the company could not immediately repay it a winding up order would be put on the business. He had come over as he had the bank directors down with him first thing in the morning and if they gave the order for the wheels to be put in motion, they were unstoppable unless we immediately came up with the money. I said that just securing the overdraft wouldn't help us and that if he expected our co-operation we would need the overdraft to be increased so that we could have some working capital. I explained about the crane deal I had just secured in Eastern Europe and how the commissions we would receive later in the year would clear any overdraft. On the strength of that we would need at least a facility of £50,000. He said that if Mike Jones and I were prepared to sign the personal guarantees he would arrange it. I then phoned Mike Jones up and asked him to come over. When he arrived the whole thing was explained to him again and I then asked Geoffrey to excuse us whilst Mike & I went into the kitchen to discuss our predicament. We were in a very precarious situation but there was no doubt that with an additional £20,000 we could continue in business and with the deal secured in Eastern Europe the personal guarantees shouldn't be too much of a risk. We went back in and said that, provided we could have the overdraft of £50,000 guaranteed for a minimum of twelve months with an option to renew at the end of that period we would be prepared to sign the guarantees. He seemed very relieved but he said that it was necessary for the guarantees to be signed immediately if we were to avoid the action of the bank directors' tomorrow morning. We asked if we could also sign the papers for the overdraft at the same time but he said, although it was only a formality, it needed to be prepared by the bank and their securities department and it would take about a week or so for all the paperwork to be sorted out but we shouldn't worry as we had his word on the matter. With that we signed the personal guarantees and we all shook hands and he was gone. It looked like we had been saved. A week or two was no time to wait and in the meantime we had the money from Schonco.

***

Two weeks passed and we had still received nothing from the bank so I tried to phone Geoffrey to find out what was happening. They told me that he was away so I asked to speak to his assistant but he too was unavailable. I tried again the next day with the same result. I was beginning to get a little worried, the money from Schonco would be running out and there would be little left after we had paid all the bills, we desperately needed that extra £20,000 overdraft facility that we had been promised. Then ten days later we received at the office a formal demand for Alban Feeds to repay the £30,000 forthwith otherwise legal action would be taken to recover the debt. We had been stitched up and lied too. The promise of the additional £20,000 on our overdraft had been given purely to extract our personal guarantees. There was never any intention of increasing our facility; all they wanted to do was secure the loan before taking action. We were given twenty-eight days to repay the money and there was no way in which we would be able to do that. The only hope we had was the commission money from the cranes and that would not be for several months. Geoffrey knew all this so why were we being pressurised now. I wrote a letter straight back explaining the promise that we had been given and showing how, in the circumstances, it was totally justified not only considering our expectations of a substantial commission towards the end of 1971 but that we had a healthy business and our normal trade would reduce any facility during the course of the trading year. I enclosed a copy of our accounts to show that we had achieved a considerable turnover and profit up until then, although in reality it did show a slight tailing off from the high point of 1969 but when all its associates were taken into the equation it was a very healthy overall picture. My letter was ignored and any attempt to contact anybody in authority at the bank was abortive – because my phone calls were never returned, therefore, I was not able to arrange a meeting.

CHAPTER 10

HELPING CHARLES SCHOENFELD

At the beginning of March I went up to see Schoenfeld at the York Street offices as I had promised to help him with his business for a couple of days a week. When I got there Jackie said that he had been taken ill and had asked if I could go round to see him at his flat in St. Johns Wood. The door was answered by his wife who said that Charles was in bed with a bronchial infection and would I go through. He looked terrible and his voice was a husky whisper. He asked me if I could run his business for him whilst he was ill. He would pay me a wage and he accepted that I still had other business commitments, but I knew his business backwards and in any case it would only be a temporary arrangement until he was better and then we could look at some other form of co-operation. I decided to be honest with him and told him of the difficulties I had with Alban Feeds which the bank would probably be forcing into liquidation and that they might well try to make me bankrupt, but that I had commission due at the end of the year that would pay off the bank. Under the circumstances it was imperative that I survive that long. In the meantime I would be only too happy to look after Schonco as long as he accepted that I still had the merchanting business to run and also that I could not desert my business partner Mike Jones. He said that he did not want Mike Jones or Mike Druce involved with his business and it was only me that he would work with. I said that I totally understood and as regards Mike Druce, I had severed all connection with him but I had a loyalty to Mike Jones. As a compromise I would run Schonco along the lines it always had and I would promote the pharmaceutical and other chemical business through it, but should it be impossible to save Alban Feeds, and that seemed very likely, I would form another company with Mike Jones to handle all feedstuff business. However to ensure that Charles did not miss out on the small amount of anti-biotic feedstuff business he was already doing he could have shares and a profit arrangement with the new company and its registered office would be with Schonco at York Street although I would continue with the Dunstable office until the lease run out and Mike Jones would work from there. He accepted all I had said and suggested that he call his solicitors, Barnet Janner Davis and Janner, to draw up the agreement and also look into my predicament for me. From his bedside phone he made the call and a meeting was arranged with Lady Morris of Kenwood, the partner in the firm who had always handled his affairs and although I had never met her before I had spoken to her when previously working for Schonco. I phoned Mike Jones to explain the situation and to be sure that he agreed, but poor old Mike was in such depths of despair that he would agree to anything. Lady Morris was charming and said that Charles had often spoken about me as he had looked on me as a son. I explained everything we had agreed and she thought it made good sense but she thought that the new company should be formed immediately to run alongside Alban Feeds until Alban Feeds was liquidated. In that way it would not appear a substitute company. I suggested that we call the company Charlfeed Ltd. and that the shareholding was split three ways, Charles, Mike Jones and me. The only caveat she said we should incorporate was that if anything happened to Charles Schoenfeld his shares would revert to me and Mike Jones. She then went on to explain that, when I had worked for Schoenfeld and also my wife earlier, he had thought very fondly of us both and considered us part of his family. So much so that he had made a will leaving everything to me as his sole heir. However when I left him he felt totally betrayed and had immediately altered his will sharing out the behests elsewhere although that was confidential. His shares would be considered part of his assets and could go to one of the other beneficiaries unless such a safeguard was made. She said that I had been foolish to discard Charles the way I did and I would have been better advised to have included him in my plans when I made my break. He was a very wealthy man and on his demise I would have had no money worries for the foreseeable future. This was especially poignant seeing my present position, but it was very unlikely that Charles would ever put me in that beneficial position again. He had been deeply hurt and told her that he would never be able to feel the same way about me and my family again although he still trusted me as a business man and would work with me, but the family feeling had gone forever. I was shocked I had had no idea of the situation then, but I told her that I fully understood and that I was happy to work with him on that arrangement and would do my best to help him. I expected nothing more than a business arrangement between friends.

***

Shortly after that Charles got better enough to come into the office and I collected him from his flat and brought him in. Under his direction Jackie and I rearranged the offices giving me a desk just outside his office in the small annex between him and the front reception area where Jackie worked. I agreed that I would spend Mondays and Fridays in Dunstable working on Alban Merchanting and sorting out Alban Feeds and the other companies and Tuesday, Wednesday and Thursday at York Street running Charlfeed and helping with Schonco. However without any co-operation from the bank the demise of Alban Feeds was inevitable and after the twenty-eight days the winding-up petition was served. Then out of the blue I received an order from L. Loria in Abu Dahbi for all the furnishings we had quoted for. The order would not solve our problems as it only amounted to a little over £2,000 and after paying a commission to Unigulf our profit was just £300. But it was a start and with the order came another enquiry for Gulf Construction also through Unigulf and that was needed at the end of May. This time I got prices from M. Hackney and telexed them out immediately and the order came by return, another £4,000 worth with a profit of just under £1,000. I had no sooner got my breath back from that when another order came through from Loria for £3,500 worth showing another £600 profit. Then the little flurry was over for a few months although Unigulf was to stay a good and constant source of business for a while. But the profits could do little more than cover our on going expenses. Only big business like the cranes would be enough to pay off the bank

***.

CHAPTER 11

FACE TO FACE WITH MIKE DRUCE

Before that and shortly after my meeting with Lady Morris I had a phone call from Jackie on a Monday morning when I was in Dunstable. Apparently Mike Druce had phoned to ask her if she had received any post for Charles Druce, especially a small parcel that he understood had been sent to York Street. As it happened Jackie said that there was some post which she had collected up from the hallway but no parcel. He then asked whether she could drop it round to his flat in Molyneux Street after work by which time the parcel may have arrived. She said that she would see what she could do and then she had immediately phoned me. I suggested that Mike and I would come up to London and take the post round to him as we would like to have a long chat with him, we needed to know what had been going on. At five o' clock we collected the post from Jackie and went round to Druce's flat in Molyneux Street. We rung the bell and Mike Druce, assuming it was Jackie, pushed the button to open the door and invited her up. When we opened the door to his apartment he looked totally shocked to see us, the colour drained from his face and for a moment he looked as if he wanted to make a bolt for it, but he soon recovered his composure and said that he was going to get in touch with us as he had only just got back and wanted to know what on earth was going on. I was finding it hard to keep my cool and I could feel the anger welling up within me. Mike Jones had taken a step behind me as if he was frightened of the confrontation that he knew was about to come. Calmly I asked him if he would like to chat to us about Inland Alkaloids, transfers of money out of Alban Feeds account, corrupt bank managers, drug hoards under floor boards and the imminent closure and collapse of a once thriving and secure business. He said that he didn't know what I was talking about, he thought that Inland Alkaloids were genuine, and as regards the money transfers, Charles Druce had been through a bad time and he had propped it by borrowing from Alban Feeds as they had been doing so well. As to the rest he knew nothing about anything and he had a right to be furious at the way we had emptied his office while he was away without even consulting him. With that I let rip, it was one of the few times I lost my temper. Virtually spitting my words out I told him how he had given Inland Alkaloids duplicate documents signed by him to collect the Ergotamine Tartrate we had kept in the warehouse, and who the " bloody hell" did he think he was, taking money out of Alban Feeds behind our back, also far more money than Charles Druce would need for running expenses. Apart from that, I was pretty sure that he had been dealing in drugs and if Charles Druce was doing so bad how could he afford his lavish lifestyle, three month holidays in Egypt, flats in one of the most expensive parts of London, flash cars and flash women. Everything I had worked for had been destroyed by him and somehow or other I was going to make him pay for it. What was worse, I thought that we had been friends and working together for the same end. The business had been enough for us all to be very rich eventually, but no, he had to swindle and lie his way through, he wanted everything now at whatever cost. He was prepared to see his business partners destitute as long as he could get away with it. He was a liar and a cheat to put it mildly, he was also a thief!

***

During my tirade Mike Druce had sat down looking at the floor and Mike Jones had edged nearer to the door. When he did eventually speak Mike Druce said that his signature must have been forged but he was sorry about the money, he really did mean to replace it. He was expecting some big orders to come through but they never materialised and he had just got carried away with everything and that's why he had run off to Egypt as he couldn't cope. He really was so sorry - he never knew it would get to this. I then told him about his little black book and the letters I had written. It was then that all the colour drained from his face completely, and a blind panic seemed to take over. He said "YOU HAVE NO IDEA WHAT YOU HAVE DONE AND WE ALL NEED TO GET AWAY AT ONCE!" I asked him what he was talking about and he had better fill us in, if everything was so innocent and the people in the book were not involved, what was it we had to worry about? He started gibbering, saying that he had to get away and anything could happen now. Then he finally calmed down, he realised he had some quick talking to do and suggested we leave the flat and go for a drink together to sort things out. I was still seething underneath and there was no way in which I could be sociable with him. I didn't believe his stories and was sure he was culpable. I suggested (foolishly in hindsight) that we all meet up at our Dunstable office the next day, then we would go through all the paperwork together and sort out what could be done to try to save everything. I also asked him to make sure that he brought with him the Charles Druce account books. He said that he would definitely be there. We left his flat with him following, I could not even walk with him and shot ahead, intending to return to the office, but as I looked back, I saw Mike Jones and Mike Druce walking together, Druce tall and angular with his floppy black hair, stooping down to Mike Jones, who was quite short. Were they going to the pub together? I was shocked to see that not only was Mike Jones was able to walk with him, but I could hear him making small talk. They were discussing Druce's holiday in Egypt, and they chatted together as if nothing had happened. I was amazed, here was a man who had destroyed our business and our livelihoods for his own selfish and greedy ends, and Mike Jones was treating him like a buddy, before we met up with Druce, he claimed he was going to rip him apart. Such are the quirks of human nature.

***

That was the last we ever saw of Mike Druce, he had given up his flat, apparently he had just been clearing out his things that night, and it appeared that he had even moved his home address. His telephone lines were disconnected and we never heard from him again. The police couldn't find him and we realised that this was something we were not going to be able to repair. The beginning of the snakes rearing their ugly heads.

CHAPTER 12

NO IDEA OF THE DANGER I WAS IN

Then came the phone calls, innocuous at first, in response to my demand letters. Initially a call went through to our Dunstable office where we had two Dutch secretaries at that time. Ann Fabretti had reluctantly left when our circumstances changed, we were unable to keep paying her the sort of money she could command. I had replaced her with Meija Dowd, a friend of Leda, who had worked for Mike Jones.
***
The phone call was from a Lester Friedman who was staying in the Royal Lancaster Hotel in London, with Nick Sands, (whom I had met in San Francisco). The message wa that they both needed to speak with me urgently. As I was already in London with Schonco, I asked Mieja to call him back and tell him that I would meet them both that afternoon, at a time convenient to them. I was curious, as they had both been on my mailing list, (found in Mike Druce's little black book), and so I was definitely interested to see their response. It was arranged that I should meet them at the hotel at 4 pm, and I was to go straight up to their suite. I arrived punctually and Nick Sands, introduced me to Lester Friedman. He was a Chemistry Professor at the University of California, and I was told that he was very highly respected. Lester Friedman then said that he had received a letter from me and wanted to know what all this nonsense was about. I then explained what had happened with Inland Alkaloids and the Ergotamine Tartrate that was sent, with their seeming connection. I went on to describe how it had destroyed my business and was about to make me bankrupt, I added that I intended to pursue the matter until I got some satisfaction. Lester Friedman denied all knowledge of the matter but said that he sympathised with my predicament. He did not see what he could do, but perhaps when he got back to the States he would make

some enquiries for me. Nick Sands had remained quiet throughout.

***

Lester then went into another room and Nick Sands turned on me. He said that I wasn't as innocent as I made out, that I had taken money from Billy Hitchcock when I was in America for a consignment that was never delivered. I denied it completely, saying that the only money I had from him was to set up an animal feed business, it was a legitimate loan legally endorsed. This matter had ruined the animal feed business, and it was now unlikely that I could pay Billy his money back which upset me, Billy had been so generous. Nick Sands looked puzzled, I think he could see I was genuine and was trying to remember what happened when Druce had taken me to meet them all.. He asked me "what about Mike Druce in all this?" I told him how I thought that he was implicated in the Inland Alkaloids affair. I went on to outline what had happened, the row I had with him, followed by his mysterious disappearance. I went on to explain how I had found he had been swindling money out of my company, Nick said that he felt sorry for me but that there was nothing he could do to help me. Perhaps I should just put it down to bad judgement and bad company and forget the whole thing; he couldn't see how I was going to get anywhere. I told him that wasn't an option, I had lost everything and my only way of surviving was to track down who was behind Inland Alkaloids order and if I couldn't do it myself then I would have to go to the police. During this conversation Lester had come back into the room and I then said there was no point in me outstaying my welcome since neither of them seemed to be able to help me, I requested that if something came up later, to get in touch with me, as time was of the essence. I then thanked them both for seeing me, shook hands and left. It was obvious they knew something, as why else would they have travelled to London specifically to see me, they could have just ignored my letters or written a reply.

***

About a week later I had the first of the phone calls at home. It was about 11.30 p.m. and I had gone to bed. I went down to answer it and a voice at the other end said that they had heard I was making trouble and if I persisted it would be the worse for me. I tried to explain that all I wanted was my money back. The next night I had another call a little after 1am. The same voice said that they knew where I lived with my wife and children. If I did not back off something really bad might happen. I asked them if they were behind Inland Alkaloids scam with Mike Druce, and if they were, they had stolen money from me. I just wanted it back otherwise I would go to the police. Two nights later the phone rung again, this time it was 3am– I ignored it. It rang again at 5 am, I continued to ignore it. The next night the same thing happened. Jan said that she couldn't put up with this all the time and that I had better answer it. I just told her that I was doing some business in America and the fools over there had no idea of the time difference. I didn't want her to be worried or ask more questions. When it rang the following night I went down to answer it. A voice on the other end said that I had been warned and if the matter went to the police, then I would be a dead man and also my family had better watch out. I was so furious, now they threaten my family, I thought it was just to frighten me but decided to keep alert anyway. In my anger I pulled the telephone straight out of the wall and snapped the wires. At least I wouldn't be getting anymore nasty phone calls. In the morning I told Jan I had tripped over the wire. She was unconcerned as she hated the disruption the telephone caused to our quiet evenings.

***

A couple of mornings later when I called into the Dunstable office Meija told me that there had been a call from someone calling himself " Professor Ronald Stark" and he had requested that I meet him at the Army and Navy club in Pall Mall at 3 o'clock the following afternoon. When I arrived the next day, it was a typical plush gentleman's club where one felt you had entered a time loop and ended up in a late Victorian establishment. It had a marbled floor entrance and high columns supporting an ornate ceiling. The commissioner showed me through to a large oak panelled room with a high ceiling hung with chandeliers, an oak floor covered with expensive Chinese carpets, large Chesterfield armchairs and settees, with side tables, and a large marble fireplace on the far wall, with a fire flickering, paired with, high backed antique armchairs on either side. As I entered a rotund man in his early fifties with a round face, thick black hair and dark swarthy skin walked over to me. He was shorter than me and had a Mediterranean appearance, he was exceptionally well dressed but in a rather loud striped suit and as he flashed me a smile I saw a glint of gold teeth. He shook my hand and motioned me to one of the two chairs in the far corner of the room, at the same time requesting the commissioner to bring two cups of coffee and some biscuits. He introduced himself as Professor Ronald Stark and said that he had been requested to meet me by friends who had been disturbed by some letters I had written. He asked me politely if I could explain what had happened. I told him the whole story of an unknown to me company, by the name of Inland Alkaloids; and Mike Druce's treachery which lead to the destruction of our business, with possible bankruptcy to follow. He listened patiently and when I had finished he shook his head saying that it was a most distressing business. He said that he wasn't without influence and with my permission perhaps he could talk to the bank on my behalf. He knew people in high places and he thought that my bank manager behaved disgracefully. If nothing else he said, if they tried to take action against the guarantees, we should counter sue, as they had been falsely extracted from us. He asked me to take no action and to leave things with him. He would also make investigations to get to the bottom of Inland Alkaloids – but his " clients" had nothing to do with it he assured me, and he strongly suspected that the names in Mike Druce's book were unlikely to be involved. His theory was that Inland Alkaloids was probably a creation by Druce's to enable him to make the collection from the warehouse, while he was supposedly in Egypt. I was getting weary of the whole affair and concerned after all the threats I had received. If he could sort out the bank and give us breathing space then I could try to resurrect something out of the ashes.

***

It was probably too late to save the feed supplement business as we hadn't paid Frank Wright all we owed and Mike Jones had failed to pacify them. Instead they had gone to a competitor, Colburn Vitafeeds, and given them our formulas. It was part spite and part survival, for if we went down, they could still continue with their business. Coburn Vitafeeds had already moved in on most of our customers who had not been able to get their usual supplies from us. In my heart I knew that I would never catch up with what was behind Inland Alkaloids and it might be dangerous involving the police. I just wanted to survive and be shot of the whole mess. Stark was very polite and pleasant. I finished my coffee and with assurances that he would do everything he could with information I had given him, I took my leave. He had read me correctly. I was to learn five years later, that he had been sent over to see if I should be eliminated, and if so, to arrange a Contract on my life. Fortunately for me, I learned later, that he had reported back to The Brotherhood, that I was small fry and as long as the organisation took preventive measures, I would probably cause them no more trouble. At the time I had no idea of this and was only to learn about it, as you will read later, through a bizarre interview in 1977 with a policeman. That was long after I had ceased to have any connection in the matter, and after several more adventures.

***

At the tender age of twenty-eight I had escaped death on the whim of one man. After that, the phone calls stopped but there was a post script to the affair several months later. Troy was on his way home from a friend's house, when a man in a car asked him to get in and he would give him a lift to meet his mother. Troy refused and ran home quickly, telling us what happened. I heard later that this had been a last attempt by a break-away section, to get even with me for the disruption I had caused. I heard nothing further from Professor Ronald Stark.

CHAPTER 13

SCHOENFELD VERY ILL/RECEIVERS MOVING-IN

Meanwhile Alban Feeds was rapidly moving to its' disintegration. The bank, having not received the payment of £30,000 they had demanded within the twenty-eight days presented us with a winding up petition which was delivered to our Dunstable office on April 10th. We now had twenty-one days to when the Receiver would take over. Promises that we had money due from other businesses were ignored and the inevitable legal juggernaut rolled on. The Receiver moved in on the 2nd May and found that the only tangible asset Alban Feeds had was my Triumph Vitesse that I had foolishly left in the company name, Mike Druce's car was owned by Charles Druce Ltd. and Mike Jones had put his car in his wife's name, although the company had purchased it. The office accommodation was rented, as was the furniture and Remdex, the leasing company agreed to switch the lease to Alban International Trading Company Ltd. (Alban ISO) which had been formed to hold our shares in Alban Feeds Ltd. which in turn held shares in all the associated companies, except for Alban Merchanting Ltd. The idea had been to transfer all the shares held by Alban Feeds in Charles Druce, Alban Produce, Guinness Chemical Company, Alban Press, Alban Securities, C & G Packaging, Eastbury Chemicals & D.&M Hair Fashions to Alban ISO but, with everything that had been going on we hadn't got around to it. Alban Feeds also held shares in a company called Connaught Cycles which had been our latest acquisition at the end of 1970. This was a business started by Mike Jones' brother-in –law to develop and market a revolutionary motorbike. It held design patents in the UK and the USA and we had put start-up capital into it. The only companies we had got around to making solely owned by Alban ISO had been Alban Merchanting Ltd. and Advikon, the name of the office in Prague run by Derek Parkhouse, which worked on introductory commissions. Consequently all the shares held by Alban Feeds in these respective companies were offered by the Receiver at a nominal cost to the other shareholders. Therefore all the businesses I had a hand in starting up ended up this way:

Alban Produce became solely owned by Les Crowther,
Alban Securities by Gordon Marshom,
Guinness Chemical Co. by Nick Nicholls,
C & G Packaging & Eastbury Chemicals by Don Longhurst & Nick Nicholls,
D & M Hair Fashions to Mike Jones's wife,
Connaught Cycles to his brother-in-law
Mike Druce got back Charles Druce Ltd.

Nobody took up the shares in Alban Press and as Alban Feeds was the majority shareholder the receiver sold off the assets when no one came forward to buy the company. Mike Jones and I were left with Alban ISO (Alban Merchanting), Advikon and of course the newly formed Charlfeed with Charles Schoenfeld.

***

At least we had managed to salvage the large commission due from American Hoist & Derrick Company which I had negotiated in the name of Alban Merchanting and the trickle of business from the Gulf. If we could tread water until then we would have a large capital base again. Ironically we received our first payment from the Gulf into Alban Merchanting two days after the Receiver took over Alban Feeds

***

In amongst all of this Charles Schoenfeld fell ill again with a stroke and Jackie, his secretary announced that she was leaving to go back to New York. In a desperate attempt to salvage things for him, I asked my sister in to help him with his secretarial work. I was sharing my time between Dunstable, the office in York Street and Schoenfeld's flat in St. John's Wood, there I was not only having to help with his office work but to act as his nursemaid as well, helping him to the toilet, cleaning him up and helping him to feed. He was convinced that he was going to get better

and I suggested that when he did it would be convenient if I had a car to take him to and from the office and for any other errands. I explained my car had been repossessed by the Receiver for Alban Feeds and I was having to go back and forth by tube and train which was time consuming. In actual fact I was using the Ford Escort which was nominally Jan's, but was still very unreliable with its intermittent fault that caused the engine to in-explicably cut out at the most awkward moments. My sister had a friend, Janet Gawn, and she was driving a fascinating little sports car that had just been made by her boyfriend, Don Finlay, in his workshop on the Isle of Wight. He had a fibreglass factory there where he made boats and remodelled cars and he had given it to her to sell on the mainland. It was he who had made the fibre glass top for my Vitesse. For this car he had used an MGB chassis and raised the suspension fitting a shortened version of an E-type body on top with a Perspex bubble roof. It was navy blue and had two front seats and a small bench seat at the back. I really wanted this car from the moment I first saw it, but in my present circumstances there was no way I could afford to buy it. It was entirely impracticable for Schoenfeld of course, but I had less confidence in his recovery than he did and he would probably never see it; so I told him that I had found an ideal run-about car to chauffer him around in when he felt a bit better, and in the meantime I could use it to run back and forth looking after his affairs. When I explained this to him he agreed to this, and much to my delight I was able to purchase it. I used to think I was the cat's whiskers running around in my little sports car in my expensive hand tooled leather coat.
***

In June and July we had another flurry of orders from the Gulf, this time Bahrain and it was for Kings Caterers, again an introduction from Unigulf. This time there were several orders from them over the two months totalling over £12,000 plus a little one from someone in Qatar called A. Vareta for £750. I split the order over several suppliers and one of them was a job buyer called Georgie who specialised in buying bankrupt stock. He was a colourful individual who had once bought a whole dry dock for scrap but I learnt later that there was a darker side to his character. He had once been bankrupted and the company was now in his wife Jessie's name. When the police swooped on his yard and discovered stolen goods, it was Jessie who had to go to prison as the owner of the company. Although Georgie ran it all and Jessie was little more than a figure head, he was quite content to step aside and let her do the time. However, despite that set back their marriage seemed to have survived and when I met them Jessie was very much in the picture. Maybe she had decided that in future she needed to know everything that went on. Anyway I managed to get everything delivered by the end of August and we received another £3,000 profit. We were still struggling through.

CHAPTER 14

TIME OFF FROM WORRIES

The next thing I needed was a family holiday.. After I had been looking after Schoenfeld and his business for a while, I told him that I needed a holiday and that I would fix up for a home nurse to look after him while I was away. As for the business, it was always quiet in the summer months and I would ask my sister to look after things whilst we were away. I would keep in contact with her in case of an emergency. Under the circumstances there was little else he could do but agree, so the first week in September we were off. We packed everything in the little sports car and headed off for North Wales – the Lleyn Peninsula. The holiday was idyllic and the weather was glorious, sunshine everyday. For the first week we stayed bed & breakfast at a little farmhouse in Llanbedra and spent all day until the sun sank low on the beach at Shell Island, and then we would find a little restaurant for dinner before we all went back to our farmhouse. Mark and Troy were little angels and so perfectly behaved that people complimented us in the restaurants and on the beach. Then at the weekend we stayed in bed and breakfast at a smart little bungalow run by an elderly couple called Harold and Mary which just happened to be the name of our ex-Prime Minister and his wife.

***

For the second week we found a little terraced cottage in Dolgellau where we could be self-catering. It was owned by an elderly lady who lived next door to it. It was a little dark and old fashioned and not very smart but it suited us. We moved in and after unpacking we went off to the beach as usual returning just as it was getting dark. After washing the children and putting them to bed we decided to get to bed ourselves. It was a very dark night and in the little bedroom we were soon fast asleep. However, in the early hours we were woken by the sound of heavy breathing that seemed to be there with us in the room. I jumped out of bed

and put the light on, but we could see nothing and the breathing had subsided. Jan said that it must be our imagination or something outside, so we got back to sleep, an hour later we were woken by the noise again and this time there was no mistaking it. Along with the heavy breathing there was a snorting and snuffling sound and it seemed to be there with us in the room. I thought that maybe the sound was playing tricks on our ears, perhaps it was the children in the next bedroom or, a much worse possibility that someone had got in downstairs. I looked in on the children but they were sleeping peacefully and I searched downstairs but there was no sign of anybody. Then the noise subsided again and we were left in silence, but in the silence if you strained you ears you could just hear the unmistakable sound of breathing. There was nothing we could do. Jan & I cuddled up in bed and had a fitful sleep interspersed with that horrible sound. In the morning daylight, I decided to investigate. Looking at the house from the outside I could just see that it had originally been one large cottage that had been divided into two and there was a window projecting slightly above our front door over which was our bedroom. I went back upstairs and there in the corner I could see the edge of the window frame and a gap between that and the partition wall separating us from the house next door where the elderly woman lived. The window had a frame slightly projecting into our bedroom, that must be her bedroom window we supposed, and her bed must be up against the partition wall. The sound we could hear was her breathing and snuffling in her sleep and it sounded so loud in our bedroom because it was coming through the small gap between the window edge and the wall. Having solved the mystery we slept more soundly afterwards, although we still had to put up with being woken up by the occasional loud snoring.
***
Just before we went home we made a visit to Carmarthen and the Castle. I bought Mark and Troy some crab lines and they did some crab fishing off the end of the jetty. They caught two large crabs and one small one which they put in

their buckets and Jan and I sat lazing in the sun. Then the time came to leave so I asked them to throw the crabs back and put the buckets in the boot of the car and we drove back to the cottage to pack for an early start the next morning. As we were driving home to Harpenden I could hear this funny scratching noise coming from the side of the car. I got out to investigate but could see nothing. It seemed to persist all the way home but it was impossible to tell exactly where it was coming from. At one time it seemed to be at the front of the car and then it seemed to come from the back. I thought that there must be something stuck to the bottom of the car and I would have to investigate when we got home. Back at Harpenden we were unpacking the car when suddenly there was a shout from Troy to Mark "Our crabs have gone". I asked him what he meant as I thought they had put them back in the sea, but they admitted that they had kept them as they wanted them as pets! Then I realised what had happened, the bucket had tipped over and the crabs had crawled out and into the hollow cill of the car. There was no way that we could possibly get them out as the cill run the length of the car and there was only a tiny opening at the edge of the boot. For months we heard that sound as they crawled up and down the cill, it was quite spooky and it was amazing how long they could live without food. But eventually the noise ceased and we assumed that they had died. There was one upset when we returned. My mum and dad had been looking after our two cats but when we went to collect them, they explained that Tibby had gone missing. At first they hadn't worried as we had told how he wandered of for several days but he had now been gone over a week. They had search for him but to no avail. We put out posters and made enquiries but he never came back and we never found out what happened to him.

CHAPTER 15

AMERICAN HOIST & DERRICK/MIKE JONES AFFAIR

On my return from holiday I heard from Derek Parkhouse that the cranes had been delivered by American Hoist and Derrick Company so I sent them my commission note for £55,000. After a month I hadn't heard anything, so I sent a chase up letter. I received a letter in reply from them saying that they did not recognise my involvement. I immediately responded with copies of our Contract and the letters I had received from their London office. To this, the response was shattering, they claimed that the London office had no authority to make such arrangements as all matters appertaining to Eastern Europe were dealt with through their Zurich office and as far as they were aware, I had received no permissions from them to pursue any business in Eastern Europe on their behalf. I pointed out that they had accepted orders which I had negotiated and that the work I had done on their behalf brought them the business that they had, otherwise they would have had nothing.
***

This was unbelievable, I had made all the contacts and presentations, which had been agreed to with a contract signed by Mike Harris, their London Managing Director, from which they received a lucrative order and agreed to my commission. All I got in reply was a curt note saying that Mike Harris was no longer with their company and the London office had been closed. Anything Mike Harris had arranged with me had been on his own account and without the authority of American Hoist and Derrick Co. They knew nothing of my involvement and there was no way that they could recognise an agent's commission in this venture.
***

By now I was getting desperate. Without this money I was completely broke and if the bank exercised their personal guarantee I would lose everything including my house. I said that at the very least I was due a finder's fee of 1% but they said that there was no proof that I found the business. In desperation I tried to contact Jaroslav Zdenek for him to verify my participation but he did not answer my letters or phone calls. I asked Derek Parkhouse to go and see him for me. Eventually Derek managed to meet up with him but Zdenek said that he had a nice little arrangement going with American Hoist and Derrick Co. and he would not jeopardise it to help me. Confidentially, Derek said that Zdenek was worried that if they recognised me they might want to cut back on his take.

***

I could do nothing I had no money to sue and anyway it would probably have to be through the American courts and that was prohibitively expensive and could go on for ever. This was my first brush with American business ethics but unfortunately it was not to be my last.

***

The business had now been paired down to a skeleton staff. I ran the London office by myself and occasionally Jan would come up with the boys and help type a few letters and at one time Mike Druce's old secretary Maxine came to work for me for a few months to help out as she was between jobs. I would have liked to have kept her on permanently but the way things were it was impossible to make any long term commitments or to pay her the sort of salary she could command. In Dunstable we had let Meija go and that office was run by Mike Jones and Leda Gilham. What I didn't know at the time was that they were having an affair. Once when I was in the Dunstable office Leda had come on to me, and I had also seen her flirting with one of the guys from the detective agency that we had sub-let the flat to as offices. She was a single parent with a boy of about four and I think she was looking for someone to share her life with. Mike Jones was not an obvious candidate as he wasn't a lady's man, he had been faithfully married for twenty years to his first girlfriend and had never even thought of straying, whereas Leda was a tall, slim, striking blond with quite a masterful way about her.

Apparently the affair had been going on for some time and Mike's wife, Val, knew nothing about it. Mike found it hard to handle all the pressure and in Leda he could escape and forget about everything else that was going on, leaving it to me to sort everything out. But he was getting deeper and deeper involved with her, and just after Christmas he was to leave his wife and children and move in with Leda. As he left Val at Eaton Bray, he at least had the decency to leave his car with her, but this meant he was without transport. So I lent him, with Jan's permission, the Ford Escort which she still refused to drive. Unfortunately, he was out in it one day when Val spotted him and followed him back to Leda's bungalow. Having found out where he was now living, she returned that night with a hammer and smashed up the Ford Escort, breaking all the windows and lights and denting the bonnet, thinking it was Mike Jones's car.

CHAPTER 16

JAN PREGNANT/FRIENDLY NEIGHBOURS

That Christmas Jan and I spent quietly at home. As usual we invited Jan's mum and dad over and visited mine. When we first moved into Harpenden things had been difficult for Jan. It was an expensive estate. Our neighbours were mostly professional people, solicitors, bank managers and executive's salesman, the youngest wife was a good fifteen to twenty years older than Jan. They had worked their way up the ladder to achieve what they had. Jan's initial shyness was misinterpreted as being unfriendly. She was never invited to the various coffee mornings they would have with each other, and she would watch them going to and fro from each other's houses. This increased her initial loneliness, however, as time wore on and Jan would meet up with them at the school she gradually formed friendships although there was little compatibility. As for Mark and Troy, they had no such trouble and they had made lots of friends. Also they went to a really good Sunday school that was forever taking all the children out on trips to the seaside or countryside or theme parks. It was supported by members of a particular church to which neither Jan or I belonged, and the church members paid for everything. They wanted nothing from us. We appreciated very much their generosity.

***

That New Years Eve we were invited to a party at our neighbours across the road; they were a Scottish couple and had just adopted a baby. We went across after we had put Mark and Troy to bed and took it in turns to pop back to see that they were alright. While I was gone they asked Jan what I did for a living as they were all fascinated because I didn't seem to fit into their accepted pattern. For a moment Jan was stumped then she remembered a conversation we had some time ago and she told them I was an entrepreneur, which didn't really answer their question but as she didn't expand on it, they decided it would have to do. The neighbours in the house immediately opposite hours said that when they saw Jan come round to the front of the house one day they thought she had no trousers on. It was some time before they realised that she was wearing beige, flesh coloured slacks and it was some time before Joe, the husband could be dragged away from the window. Dee, his neighbour, said that Sid, her husband was always ogling out the window whenever he saw Jan especially in her mini-skirts. All of this made Jan blush and giggle, but neither of us had realised how much attention has been focused on us through those net curtains.

***

Early in January, we found that Jan was pregnant. We had talked about having another child as she would like a little girl to go with the two boys we had, both of whom would soon be at school, Mark having already started and Troy was now spending three days a week at nursery school and the following year would start at 'big school'. Jan had thought that now would be a time for an addition to the family, but soon she felt that things weren't quite right and as things progressed she became more convinced that this baby wasn't like the others. She had a feeling of bloating quite early and she had much more sickness than before. She was sure something was wrong and then one night when I helped her to bed with a nice hot drink to calm her, she woke up with terrible stomach pains. The next minute she rushed to the toilet and she explained later, that she felt as if everything gushed from her. We called our doctor who told us Jan had just lost the baby. But Jan had a sense of relief, as she said that she had never felt happy because she was convinced that if the baby had been born it would have had some terrible deformity. The doctor checked her over, and apart from a discomfort in her tummy she was essentially well and psychologically she accepted the situation as a necessary termination.

CHAPTER 17

SCHOENFELD DIED

A couple of months after Christmas Charles Schoenfeld died and I received a note from Lady Morris asking if I could deal with matters at the flat as Lena, Charles's wife, had gone to a nursing home. I was to arrange for a house clearance as soon as the funeral was over and the proceeds of sale were to go to the estate. All items of value had already been taken by Scheonfeld's brother Lasar and what was left was to be disposed of probably through a second-hand furniture dealer. When I looked over the flat, apart from the furniture there was a large coloured television, something I knew Jan would love as we only had a small black & white one. Lasar had taken everything he thought of value and obviously he had not thought the television worth bothering with. There would be little value in it from the house clearance so I thought that perhaps I should have it, so I took it home. Jan was delighted and it was amazing to watch our favourite programs on such a big screen and in colour. The only trouble was that a couple of months later I had a phone call from a television rental company asking if I had noticed a television amongst Mr. Schoenfeld's effects when I was clearing the house as it was essential that the television was traced as it was their property. I said that I would do what I could to see if I could find it for which they thanked me greatly. Several phone calls later they were becoming very irate and were threatening to report the matter as it had to be found. I told them that I thought maybe one of his relatives may have it or perhaps one of the domestics that looked after the Schoenfelds and that I would make a point of visiting them all to locate it and could they give me all the details including the serial number. Again they profusely thanked me for all my trouble. Lo and behold I then contacted them to say that I had located it and would be bringing it back to their shop. They thought I had been so diligent on their behalf and could not thank me enough. When I took the television back I said that it seemed a very good set and would they consider selling it. They said that I had been so helpful they would let me have it at a special price which was a fraction of their normal selling price for used sets. I paid for it and much to Jan's delight returned with the television set.

***

But at work troubles were accumulating. Alban Feeds had gone and most of its associated companies were continuing to thrive under their individual owners, but I no longer had any connection with them. Schoenfeld had died but the rent on 94 York Street had been paid until the end of the first quarter 1972 and I could continue running Charlfeed from there. Dr. Soloman had inherited Schonco and he wanted it phased out. He said that he would put no money into it and it would have to cease after the present contracts and stock had run out. He wanted me to give him an assessment of its current position and let him have all the books. Any surplus money should be paid to DDSA Pharmaceuticals as would any profits. He would pay no wages to me or any secretary after the end of the month. My only benefit was to be free office accommodation until the end of the first quarter. I could continue to rent the offices if I wished after the end of that period but I would have to pay for them myself. In addition I was committed to the rent at Dunstable and the wages there, Leda Gilham and Mike Jones. Cormac Martin had already decided to leave at the first hint of trouble. I had to earn something myself if only to cover the mortgage and weekly bills and I could no longer afford to keep my on anyone as secretary, I would have to try to run the London office by myself. It was going to be very difficult. I knew that I would never get the commissions I had thought would solve all my problems from the cranes, the Gulf business had dried up and the animal feeds business had been lost with Frank Wrights co-operation to Coburn Vitafeeds. There would be no income from the previously associated companies and I felt a little cheated with Soloman's attitude as I had given up time and effort to support Schonco during Schoenfelds illness only to lose everything. I had to generate money somehow. Looking through Schonco's books I saw that the Ascorbic Acid I had sold him had gone to DDSA but the sale of Chloramphenicol had not gone through, but although it was not on his stock records, it must still be in stock in Hamburg. I quickly adjusted the paperwork to let it remain in Charlfeeds possession. At least the sale of that would cover costs for a month or so. I then completed the assessment and records and delivered them to Dr. Soloman. After that I wrote to Drokasa, the buyers in Peru, offering them the Chloramphenicol in the name of Charfeed, explaining that it was an associated company. But that was only tickling the problem. Apart from trying to build up trade through Alban Merchanting and rekindle some chemical and feedstuff business through Charlfeed I had no other long term plan. I had no capital to buy stock to continue the chemical trade, although I might be lucky enough to do one or two back to back transactions but the business climate had slowed down considerably. Then came the blow I had been dreading. The personal demands for repayment from the bank under the personal guarantees we had signed. They wanted immediate repayment of £30,000 plus interest or our proposals to deal with the debt. I decided that I would have to consult Lady Morris, Schoenfeld's old solicitor who I had already told the background story. She put me in touch with Norman Shine, a partner in the business who was more of a specialist in litigation as in her opinion, endorsed by Norman Shine, we should counter sue the bank for not only allowing an unauthorised overdraft without consultation but also extracting fraudulent guarantees under false promises.

***

In March Jan's brother Colin got married and I was his best man. His bride was a very pretty brunette named Sally and Jan was to be one of her bridesmaids with Sally's sister Penny the other one. I had become good friends with Colin since the early days when I had been courting Jan. Then I had paid him to go to the pictures to leave us alone but I had also introduced him to my music taste, getting him

hooked on Ray Charles amongst others. As time wore on he would talk to me about his work and when he was working for a large company he was offered a job with a small grain brokerage company. He remembers my advice then that it was much better to be a big fish in a small pool that a small fish in a big one. Later when he and three friends were talking about setting up by themselves I did all I could to encourage him and the four of them became very successful. One other thing he always remembered me saying was that the only thing to fear in life was a painful death everything else however bad or traumatic could be coped with eventually. I was always philosophising. I remember in a discussion with Jan and some friends, when they said that they really envied someone and wished they had their life, that to really want that you had to wish that you were that person with their personality and back life and everything that made them what they were, you couldn't just pick the bits you liked. Anyway Sally, Colin's bride had worked as a reporter on the Surrey Comet and lived on a houseboat in Kingston. She was intelligent and good company and we all got on well together. I took my job as best man seriously and did all I could to make things run smoothly. Jan looked beautiful as a bridesmaid and she had dieted to lose weight to try to match Penny who was extremely slim. At the wedding one of Sally's aunts asked who was the pretty little bridesmaid and was told it was Colin's sister she said "It can't be she was a plump little thing and besides she's not old enough to have children." Jan was amused when she heard that and said all the months of dieting were worth it by learning about that comment. I made my speech at the reception, and all went well.
***

CHAPTER 18

GRASPING AT STRAWS

Norman Shine was an extremely large, rotund man with a big moon face and glasses. He was very down to earth and was interested to hear all that I had done prior to this predicament. He said that he thought that we had a good case against the bank but he could keep the ball in play whilst I got back on my feet and accumulated some money. He said that he had lots of contacts that he could put me in touch with and with my approach to business there were many lucrative deals to be done in the general merchanting field. The first person he suggested I meet was his brother-in-law, Jack Joseph and he arranged for me to see him on the coming Friday evening. I told Jan that I might be late home and turned up at Jack Joseph's house in Mill Hill a little after 7.00 pm. Jack Joseph was a market trader and still had a stall in Petticoat Lane, with him was another man called Mike Newman who was in property as well running a fabric shop. We got on well straight away and our conversations ranged from job buying and barter trading through to the uselessness of estate agents. It was on this last point that I started to develop my theory of a property shop where one building would house an estate agency and mortgage brokerage, architects, conveyance clerks, wall coverings, paints, fabrics and wall & floor tiles, carpet samples and other items for the home with brochures on the larger furnishings and kitchen design. As well as this it would have a directory of local approved tradesman who could do plumbing, electrical work and any other alterations needed. Therefore when someone came into the Property Shop they could be shown houses and any items they needed to improve and furnish it with costings and quotes for any alterations. In addition they could arrange their mortgage and their purchase all under the one roof. It was an idea I was to nurture and gradually work towards over the next few years. But on a more immediate note they

suggested that I should involve myself in general home and export trading using bankrupt or clearance stock which would give me a quick turnover and profit and handled correctly I would use the minimum of capital as I would back to back the deals sometimes using a third party as nominee. In this respect they would introduce me to a whole raft of people who would be useful to me and one big asset I had was a good trading address at 94 York Street. It was nearly 3.00 a.m. by the time I left. I had phoned Jan at about 10.30.p.m. to say that I might be late but I never expected it to go on that long and when I got back Jan was fast asleep. I quietly got undressed and slipped into bed, not waking her but giving her a gentle kiss on her lips. It was from this point that the kaleidoscope of characters and events that I referred to earlier started, with one introduction leading to another sometimes beneficial and sometimes a waste of time and money and at the same time I was trying to regenerate the business on Charlfeed. I will try to catalogue events as I remember them but at the same time I was trying to contain the overspill into my home life.
***

Following my meeting with Jack Joseph & Mike Newman various characters started turning up at York Street. The first person I remember was Jim Davis, an associate of Mike Newman, who supplied market traders with various surplus and bankrupt stock items. He was a large, burly, elderly man with a ruddy face, thinning grey hair and a cockney accent. He looked like what he was, a market trader and he was constantly introducing items that he said were so cheap we would be foolish not to buy them. Amongst the goods offered were several boxes of paper towels and a range of talcum powder. Apparently the factory that made the latter were going bust and he said that we should take over their stock and look at taking over the production line as, with our own labelling and design there was always a market for inexpensive talcum powder. The paper towels we managed to sell on a back to back basis with a small profit and with that I said I would buy a case of the talcum powder to see how it would sell before looking at whether we should be involved in production. Suffice to say that several years later I still had most of that case left. Then one day he introduced me to his brother, Sacha Davis. You could not have two brothers more different. Sacha was suave and debonair with silver grey hair and several gold teeth when he smiled which was a crocodile smile. He was well spoken and he had several expensive rings on his fingers, but his talk was soft, persuasive and slightly unctuous. He had all the air of a smooth confidence trickster. He dealt in much larger and more expansive projects, well away from the market goods of his brother Jim and what he wanted to talk about was a large crane and construction company in Holland, Munsters Machinenfabrik, which was going bust and could be purchased for a song and he had just the person who could possibly back this. The factory not only made plant and heavy equipment but also had a line in pre-fabricated houses and Sacha apparently knew where a lot of their products could be sold, especially on the African market. The next day Sacha brought a young chap round to the office who he introduced as Christopher Pike. He was in his early twenties, tall and thin with blond hair and looked like a young aristocrat. He spoke like one as well. Sacha introduced him and said that the two of us should get on well as I was a young chap full of ideas and Chris wanted to be involved in some interesting enterprise. We spoke about things generally for about an hour and then Sacha said that he was going to take him across to 'Oodles' the vegetarian restaurant that had opened just across the road. It seemed that he had only just left when Jim Davis came in; it was as if he had waited for them to come out for his cue. Jim then explained that Chris Pike was a protégé of Sacha's and was already quite wealthy but next year he was to inherit £225,000 in his own right that was currently being held in trust for him. He was looking to Sacha to find a good investment for him.

***

When Sacha and Chris returned from lunch Sacha said that they had been discussing Munsters Machinenfabrik in Holland, and Chris had suggested that we go over to see the factory and meet with the directors and invited me to go with them. We would go over in Sacha's Mercedes and Chris offered to pay our fares. We could stay overnight with friends of Sacha, in the Hook of Holland. I checked with Jan and I agreed to go on the following Wednesday as her mother would stay overnight with her at the bungalow. As to the trip itself I only have hazy memories. I was picked up from the office. Then I remember that we were accompanied by Chris Pike's brother and we stayed in a house in the middle of nowhere up in the reclaimed lands of the Zieder Zee with this middle aged couple and they also had a son of Chris's age. I remember everybody getting terribly drunk and I was sitting in the corner just drinking advocate in huge quantities. While everybody else was whooping it up I was being violently sick and then through a haze I vaguely remember the three young boys behaving like 'hooray henries' and throwing all the beds and bedding out of the upstairs window on to the lawn below whilst howling with laughter and Sacha and the older couple fast asleep in their chairs. What happened after that I can't really remember but I woke up in a small back bedroom in an armchair fully clothed and dragging myself up, the house looked like the aftermath of a battle with debris and bodies everywhere. I washed and changed and letting myself out I went for a walk in the desolate flat landscape, along the dykes to the sea wall. By the time I got back everyone was up and busy and most of the mess had been cleared up. Everyone was hung over and in a dour mood but Chris, Sacha and I had a meeting to get to so there was no time to hang around. I did what I could to help the rest of the clearing up and declined breakfast, I then said my goodbyes to the middle aged couple as I had no intention of coming back, Chris's brother could come with us and wait whilst we had our meeting. The meeting with Munsters was good and we got on very well together. I was most interested in their modular homes, the company assets had been run down and there was very little plant and equipment left and they had a buyer for what was left, but they still had everything necessary to rebuild the modular home side up and I could see a future for this in the holiday home market. Chris was quite enthusiastic. We took a lot of brochures, shook hands and said that we would be in touch. Chris, his brother and me were to fly back from Schipol airport and Sacha was going to stay on as he had other business to do. Chris and his brother slept virtually all the way back and on the bus from Heathrow, and I finally arrived home a little before midnight. After that episode I remember buying and selling various job lots. I bought some goods from Georgie Pound and sold them to someone called Donald Lewis who I remember meeting in his office in south London and if anyone looked the image of a London gangster, he did. He sat behind a large desk in a dingy back office in a striped shirt with his sleeves rolled up and his hair greased back. He wore dark glasses and a snarl on his face and drove a very hard bargain. I remember praying that nothing went wrong with the order.

CHAPTER 19

TAKING FAMILY AWAY

In between all this Jan and I managed to squeeze in a holiday with my parents down in Cornwall. I hired a Datsun Estate car to take us all, we needed to go in one car as Dad didn't want to drive all that way and both Dad's and my little sports car were too small. Anyway, we stayed in a little cottage at the end of a narrow lane on the opposite side of the A30 to Alternun. It was in the heart of Bodmin Moor next to a large forest. At the back of the cottage was a large field with cows in it and early one sunny morning I went into the kitchen and there was a cow poking its head through the open kitchen window trying to lick the draining board. Mark and Troy loved it there. While we got ready to take them to the beach they played outside with frogs they had found in the dew ponds or climbed the trees in the part of the forest where the lane ended just down from our cottage. Then we would all go off to the beach somewhere or else Jan and I would take the boys for a walk on the moors or through the forest while Mum and Dad just lazed away in the cottage. We had taken our cat Toby with us and on the way back we stopped overnight at a lovely farmhouse in Devon run by a typically buxom Devon farmer's wife. We left Toby in the car at night on his made up bed and with a small opening in the window either side. It wasn't a hot night and he looked comfortable. The farmer's wife cooked us a lovely evening meal with all produce from the farm and while we were eating it we looked across at the window and there was Toby sitting comfortably on the sill just looking in on us. Later when I went to check on him he was back curled up on his bed in the car. He was also a strange cat as he loved the rain and he would lay out spread-eagled on his back luxuriating in the pouring rain falling on him. Incidentally the farmhouse breakfast we had there was one of the best I have ever tasted.

CHAPTER 20

CHAOTIC BUSINESS & HOME-LIFE

On the business front the next twelve months were a period of total confusion with no coherent linear narrative, where shadowy figures come and go across the landscape. I can remember events but cannot put them in any meaningful order. It all coalesces into a random homogenous mass of incidents, one tumbling after another with no time frame to separate them. I will try to weave some sequence of events but with so much happening in such a short space of time no character can be guaranteed their correct time slot. I was thrashing around like some stricken animal trying to find a way to ward off the inevitable financial disaster, hanging on to the merest thread of potential business in the hope that it would lead to some substantial long term salvation. There were some business coups and some false avenues where the gains were once again lost. Throughout all this I struggled to keep my private life away from all the chaos happening in my business life. When I came home and shut my front door I was in another world with Jan, Mark and Troy. I made sure that they knew nothing of the mayhem that reigned outside and this was to remain the pattern of my life for many years. In those early days the children would rush to me as soon as I opened the front door and usually I would have to sit in judgement on some argument between them that had occurred earlier in the day. Jan would have told them "Leave it for now and we will sort it out when daddy gets home." Since they were born I was always very conscious that Jan had been having to cope by herself from the moment I left until the moment I returned. I thought then, and still do that looking after children and running the home was far more demanding than going off to work, even the stressful situations I got myself in. At least I could leave it all behind for a few hours but for Jan it was constant with little to no escape and as a wife, mother, cook and housekeeper she excelled. The children were always neat, clean and tidy and the house was always immaculate. Every day I came home to a lovely meal cooked by Jan and all the love and affection any man could ask for. She was perfect. To try to compensate I had always taken over my duties with the children when I got back from work. I would undress them and get them ready for bed while Jan cleared up and then, every night I would lay on the bed with them and tell them a bedtime story, sometimes one I had made up and sometimes from a big story book or a book of fairy tales. Then if they were disturbed in the night I would get up and see to them, I was a light sleeper anyway. Later, when we had the twins we would share the night time role. At the weekends, on a Saturday we would usually go over to St. Albans to see my parents, but in the morning and on a Sunday I would play games with them, sometimes we would be acting out stories accompanying a classical record such as 'Hall of the Mountain King' or 'Fingal's Cave' which usually involved climbing over the furniture or making hiding places behind the settee or chairs. I also later let them have my old Dancette record player and huge collection of 45 rpm records to play with. Mark attributes all the boys' love of music to the fact that all of them would play my music most of the time until they could afford to buy their own. On Sunday afternoons we always went for a walk in the countryside before coming back for Sunday dinner. These walks developed into voyages of discovery as we located obscure footpaths and relying on a sense of direction tried to make a round walk of them. This practice continued with Jan & me throughout our married life, first with the boys and as they grew up and started to live separate lives, just the two of us. We visited and saw some of the most beautiful corners of Britain as our walks continued through holidays, weekends and week days when I could escape from work.

On our return I met again with Norman Shine to make our full statements concerning the case against the bank and to issue our counter writs. He told me that the bank manager had committed suicide. He knew nothing more than that, he had not been given any reason and on a personal basis he wasn't sure how it affected our case. Our bank manager would not be there to be cross examined and to give his version of the extraction of the guarantees. Also the suicide could show him as an unstable character that could make such false promises. Then our discussions turned to the introduction he had given me to his brother-in –law and I told him about my meeting with Munsters Machinenfabrik, in Holland.

***

Norman then mentioned that he had a client in Languedoc in South of France who had land to sell and his brother-in-law knew someone who could certainly finance buying the land. At that time there was a Government scheme running called export credit guarantees and they would pay for your export order immediately and collect the money from your customer in eight months' time. What needed was for someone to set up a company in Languedoc and order the modular homes from my company in the U.K. I would then apply for export credit guarantee and pay Munsters Machinenfabriken. By the time the company in Languedoc had to pay the money up the site should be up and running and highly mortgageable. All I needed was someone to initially buy the land and then sell it as a completed holiday village.

***

A meeting was organised for me to meet a Mr. Starr. He was looking to invest some money I was told. We had a meeting room in the Grosvenor Hotel for me to meet him. When I arrived he was seated at a conference table with a secretary to take notes and what looked like two burly bodyguards behind him. After introductions, I explained my project to him, and he nodded as I went through it. He then said he liked it very much but it needed some refinements. Munsters Machinenfabriken was going bust anyway, so we should get credit from them and then let them go to the wall. The company in France, once set up will just get a lease on the land and once they had given the order and we had been paid under the Export Credit

Guarantee facility we could then wind up the company in Languedoc having first done a paper transaction to sell off the homes to another shelf company somewhere who would then sell off the goods. He then said in his soft voice "Bona. Bona, we get paid twice for the same goods and we don't have to pay for them. Can't be bad". I said that in theory it sounded as if it would work but it could be very dodgy and besides I didn't like having to cheat Munsters like that. Also if the Board of Trade found out we were swindling them I could go to prison and since it stood up as a good bona fide with the possibility of long term gains, why did we have to screw it up for a short term gain. While he had been talking I had been drinking the tea that had been served up and now I was dying to relieve myself. I looked across at him and I could see the frown on his face and the sour expression, also I could have sworn that he was cracking his knuckles. Anyway, I asked to be excused for a moment and went to the toilet. His two bodyguards followed me in and waited until I had finished rinsing my hands. Then one of them got hold of my lapels and rammed me up against the wall hissing in my ear " No-one argues with Mr. Starr, understand me?" He then let me go and followed me out into the room where Mr. Starr was angrily awaiting my return. There was no way I could work with this man so I told him that his scheme was very good, but I would be out of my depth trying to make it work. However, I was quite prepared to hand the whole thing over to him and I would make the necessary introductions and bow out. I then shook hands and left. I felt sad about it as I was in effect sacrificing Munsters and would not be able to follow through with any of my business ideas with them, but Mr. Starr was too dangerous a man to cross and once having introduced the idea to him I knew that he wouldn't let it go.

CHAPTER 21

NEED TO TRY AGAIN

Another person I met through Norman Shine was Chris Craddock at his offices down in Suffolk. His father had swindled the government out of £8 million pounds in an export credit fraud and was now on the run. He had bought an expensive yacht on which he lived and run his business through a link to his son Chris. He had to be constantly on the move always ensuring that he was in neutral or friendly waters. I was to come across him a little later. In the meantime I sold his son some miscellaneous products I had bought from Jack Joseph. One other character I remember was Maurice Posgate – a bankrupt aircraft broker who wanted me to act as a front for him. From him I bought some Beagle Pup aircraft which I then sold onto Property Management Consultants in Regent Street and another lot to someone called Michael Collins. I always remember Mike Collins. He was a chap about forty, small neat and exceptionally smart with a permanent tan. He drove a white Rolls Royce with white leather upholstery which he used to park on the pavement above the double lines outside my office. Usually when he parked there the traffic warden would come in and ask whose Rolls Royce it was. Mike would turn round tell him it was his whereupon the warden would say that he really shouldn't park there and how long will he be. To which Mike would reply only about five minutes and the warder would walk off. He never got a ticket. Such is the power of money. I had accumulated so many tickets that when the police called at my house I had to do a deal settling £200 worth of fines for £130cash. You could do such things in those days.
***

Also through Sacha Davis I met a titled baronet who was a friend of a member of the government. With him I somehow got involved in a deal to sell half-track vehicles to Numidia which I later learned was a front to get the vehicles into South Africa. As South Africa was on the embargo list it was a convenient way of getting goods in through the back door, although I didn't initially know that. I was getting mixed up in things that I didn't like and I was keeping some very dodgy company. I needed to extricate myself before I was dragged down with them. With Maurice Posgate I also got involved in aircraft broking, dealing with Curly Walters the head of BEA. On one occasion we had leased some aircraft belonging to BEA to a holiday company called Autair, who my sister had worked for at one time. In this confusing period I also somehow found time to write to a University History Professor about doing local pictorial history books showing the development of local towns and villages illustrated with maps and walks and places of interest but with an accent on the history, including reconstructions and present day photos. I got an enthusiastic response and an offer of joint co-operation but, like everything else I don't seemed to have followed it through. I also dabbled in selling car stereo equipment from Hong Kong and Taiwan to Los Angeles. They consisted of eight track cartridge players and a few tape players. Another incident I remember was luncheon I was supposed to have with Barney Keegan, one of the Directors of J.C. Bamford where I was to discuss an enquiry I had for some heavy plant. We met at the Maltings in Wheathampstead at midday. Barney was there before me and was already on his second pint. The Maltings had a wonderful display of liquors running the length of two shelves behind the bar and I ordered one of my mixtures. Not being a beer drinker I always looked at drinking as an intellectual exercise, while I tried to work out what drinks would blend with what, making up my own cocktails. Barney was intrigued by this and after a couple more drinks he asked if I could work my way through the shelves working out what went with what. After the few drinks I had already had it seemed like a challenge I couldn't resist. We never bothered with dinner as, with Barney paying, I gradually worked my way through the selection. We eventually left at around 6 pm and I'm still not really sure how I got home, but Jan said that I just walked through the door, greeted her and the children and went straight up to bed and I didn't surface until the morning. It was the only time I came back and didn't do my usual routine of helping with the chores and the next morning I was a zombie. At least Jan knew that it was a one off and when I explained the next day what had happened she just said that I was a fool but as long as I wasn't paying I could live with the consequences. However at the Maltings I had attained celebrity status. The manager had a plaque made up to celebrate the achievement, although I think that it was more of a marketing ploy to encourage others to see if they could do the same. In the end it could only be good for the profits. I later had a much more sober meeting with Barney and it was some of their plant we sold to the Gulf.

CHAPTER 22

JAN PUT HER FOOT DOWN

During most of 1972 I was like a drowning man thrashing about and clinging to anything that I thought might lead me to a way of resurrecting my business empire I had lost and what was more, creating a reserve to pay off the bank. I wasn't completely confident that we were going to succeed in our litigation; I had brushed with big business before and lost.

***

In amongst all this I remember an episode that ended up in Jan and I having one of our few blazing rows and was to change the way I was to try to do business. It was toward the end of the year Mike Jones and I decided that the only real way to resurrect our previously thriving business would be a round the world trip using up our last reserves. There was business to be had and we used to have good relations with our agents and customers that had disappeared through neglect. I was making some money from the varied business escapades I was involved in which could be invested in the trip and it could establish a more stable business that we had let slip through our fingers. I worked out an itinerary starting in Greece and Cypress and from there to the Gulf States, then across to Iran, Pakistan, India, Malaysia and Singapore, Thailand, Hong Kong, Taiwan, Japan and back via Mexico and Cuba taking in everywhere we had contacts or previous sales, except Peru which would have been too big and costly a diversion. In all the trip would take two months and it was to be our last desperate throw. As the salesman who had dealt with these people I was the obvious candidate to go, but when I told Jan, she exploded. She said that she was fed up with my gallivanting around and she felt I was starting to neglect her again. She said that she was fed up with her life at home with the children and the only thing that made it bearable was the time we spent together. I tried to be rational arguing that once the business was on an even footing I would have much more time to spend with her but it was too late she no longer wanted to hear rational argument and moderate tones only inflamed the situation worse. All her fears and loneliness and despondency over the years came to a head and she just wanted to vent everything. I was trying to back away from her but she followed me from room to room beside herself shouting and screaming at me between sobs and behind her followed Mark and Troy totally intrigued by this strange and volatile behaviour that they had never seen before. Eventually I realised that my attempts at rational argument were driving her further and further into rage and I tried to say I was sorry and hug her but she was thumping me with her flaying arms in frustration and despair. Then she collapsed sobbing in my arms and I just held her tight. When everything had calmed down I said that I would not make the trip and in future she and the family would always come before business. She was my life and I would rather walk away from everything than lose her and I meant every word of it. I told her that sometimes I let things just escalate and if ever she saw the signs of this happening again she must tell me and I would check myself. Wherever possible I would try to include her in everything. I told her that I would also try to wind down things at work, I was already worried about the 'demimonde' I was slowly being sucked into and that was why I wanted to get back to the old business of chemical and feedstuff trading I thought that this trip might resurrect.

***

Back at work I told Mike Jones that he would have to do the trip instead. I had booked everything through Lindsey Travel with accommodation at all the best hotels I had sorted out for myself including 'The Hilton' in Tehran, the Taj Mahal Palace in Bombay, the 'Raffles' in Singapore, the 'Mandarin Oriental' in Bangkok & the 'Mandarin' in Hong Kong and Taiwan and for the departure to be the second week of January, returning two months later. When originally planning it I had thought that as is was to be our last throw we should go out in style. Also, although this wasn't a business consideration, I had discovered that Leda, who Mike was living with, was having an affair with one of the private detectives in the offices above in Dunstable. I had bumped into Sandy who had been our office junior there, she was a pretty young girl married to a sailor and we had to let her go in our cull of costs after the Druce debacle. She told me that she had seen Leda with this man in the park and she had subsequently seen him going in and out of Leda's house during the day as she lived almost opposite. She said that she thought it was strange as she knew Mike was still living there. I think Sandy enjoyed such a bit of juicy gossip and had been dying to tell someone who knew all parties. Anyway, I was certain that, with Mike being away for so long, Leda would probably seize the opportunity to dump him. I had got Jan's Ford Escort back from Mike and as a part early Christmas present for Jan I traded it in for a little blue Mini which she loved. She felt at home in that little car and it got her out driving again. Jan's parents joined us again for Christmas and so did Colin & Sally. We all enjoyed ourselves and on Boxing Day it snowed heavily. Jan's Mum and Dad had gone home but Colin and Sally were snowed in with us and ended up staying almost a week before they could get home.

***

In January Mike Jones set off on his round the world trip and I took him to the airport. I noticed that Leda had not wanted to see him off, and things seemed a little strained between them. After he had gone I phoned his wife, Val, to ask if I could go and see her. I asked her if she wanted Mike back as I thought his involvement with Leda was over. I explained that I thought it was the pressure of all the mess in our business that had tipped Mike over and why he had turned to Leda as a form of escape. I also said that I thought he had been riddled with guilt at taking her and the children away from their comfortable life in Derby and exposing them to all the mayhem and uncertainty of our business, and that I blamed myself for encouraging it all. He should never have left Frank Wright and all the security it offered them. She said that she would like to try to make a go of it again but didn't know how. I told her that I would let her know on what flight he was returning and if she wanted to come with me to meet him at the airport, I thought there could be reconciliation. She said that she would think about it and give me a ring. Meanwhile Mike Jones was wending his way round the globe, apparently having a whale of a time. In a bar in Thailand he got chatted up by a beautiful Thai girl and really couldn't believe his luck. After several drinks they went up to his bedroom and started some serious heavy petting. Then to his horror he discovered that she was a man, it was his first encounter with a Thai ladyboy. He was mortified and hurriedly tried to hassle him/her out of the room, pushing and shoving him/her through the door but he/she wouldn't go quietly and when he finally managed to close the door he/she was out in the corridor hammering on the door and waking all the corridor shouting that Mike owed him/her for the service and was a cheat. Eventually the management had to take the ladyboy away and in the morning Mike got a severe lecture for allowing it all to happen. When he reached Japan he had run out of money and I had to raid the coffers to transfer some to him and two weeks later he was phoning again for more money. I sent what I could but told him that he would have to abort the trip and come home. Not only were we running out of money but we also now had a date for our pre-court hearing for the court case against the bank which was scheduled for the end of the first week of March. On the 23rd February I transferred the last of the funds out to him and told him to settle all his bills and arrange to cancel his stopovers in Mexico & Cuba and come straight back. I contacted Val and asked her if she wanted to come with me to meet him at the airport and she said that she did. When I picked her up I noticed for the first time that she looked very attractive. She had lost a lot of weight and had her hair styled in a modern cut, she really had quite a pretty face and she was dressed to the nines, overall looking years younger than I had ever seen her. Mike was shocked to see her there but I could see from his face how pleased he was. I left them for a time in the airport lounge and then I picked them up and ran them back to Eaton Bray. They were back together.

CHAPTER 23

GAMBLE DID NOT PAY OFF

However the gamble of the trip had not paid off. Mike Jones had not managed to secure any business, just a lot of vague promises and possibilities but nothing to even start to make inroads into the cost let alone the contracts I was hoping for to start building our business up. Then we had the second blow. Just before our court appearance Norman Shine was arrested for his part in the diamond fraud with Frank Craddock and placed in Wormwood Scrubs. The court hearing was adjourned and I went to see him in prison. He said that he had completed all the paperwork and was going to brief Council when all this blew up and he hadn't been able to do anything more than a short discussion. Council had needed a complete synopsis and that's what he was just doing when he was arrested. He reiterated that he thought that we had a good solid case and he was sure that the bank couldn't win. His legal team had applied for bail and he was confident that it would be granted. As soon as he was out he would sort things out with Council and we could go ahead, the trouble was that so much of the arguments he intended to use were in his head and he hadn't had chance to put everything on paper. Once he had done that the case could be delegated to someone else who would take over with Council. As he anticipated he got bail and returned home but the night he was back he had a heart attack, apparently making love to his wife as she said later, and was rushed to hospital. As I had said he was a huge man grossly overweight and never a fit specimen. On the way to hospital he had another fatal attack and was dead on arrival. The paperwork needed for Council had never been done and the special arrangement I had with Norman Shine on fees died with him. We had no money to continue the court case and although it had been adjourned for six months there was nothing we could do.

CHAPTER 24

DESPERATE TO SURVIVE

From that moment I felt like giving up. We had spent all our money on a useless trip, we had little prospect of succeeding in our case against the bank without pumping money into it. I was disenchanted with all the business I had become involved in. the latest in that line had been working with a character called Leon Morse who imported tools and pots and pans from Japan. Since Christmas I had been tramping around the department stores trying to sell this stuff, meeting some of the rudest and most ignorant people I had dealt with calling themselves buyers. Their offices were usually situated on the top floor and I would trudge to the top carrying two suitcases full of samples of heavy tools and kitchen utensils. Then after my spiel the buyer would ask to see the samples, say they were rubbish and summarily dismiss me, leaving me to trudge back down the stairs with my back breaking load. I also had a range of Barum tyres from my old acquaintances in Czechoslovakia that they had given me to sell. I managed to get an appointment to see the buyer at Fords of Dagenham. After waiting for almost an hour I was shown into his huge office where he sat behind his large desk on a high backed swivel chair. I was asked to sit down on a small chair in front of his desk. He then looked at his watch and said that I had precisely six minutes to tell him why he should buy Barum tyres starting immediately. With that he swivelled his chair so that I was facing his back. Then after I had been speaking for what I assume was six minutes he swivelled his chair back to the front and said right I'll let you know and ushered me out. The only consolation was that I got a small trial order three weeks later which I forwarded on to the Czech agency. The only decent buyer I met was a young chap in Welwyn Garden City Stores who was pleasant to me and gave me my first order. I met with him regularly and he was always friendly. Later in the year, when my car was still in the garage and we were having trouble with Jan's mini just before we were going on holiday he lent me his car for the week, a Vauxhall Viva, for which I was very grateful.

***

Two other projects I started during this period were to rumble on in the background for many years and both I ended up giving away to the other people involved with me. The first was with a man, Mike Lovett-Williams, I had known during my chemical trading period and who at this time was working with Nick Nicholls. He contacted me to ask if he could work with me to resurrect the animal feed business. He knew from Nick of my troubles and said that I could use his office in Reading as a base and his secretary would work with me. These expenses would be set against any profit which would be split 50:50 afterwards. The idea was attractive as it would allow me to give up the expensive York Street office and also when the lease run out at Dunstable I need not renew it. The only trouble was I believed the animal feed business for us was dead especially after Mike Jones's abortive trip. We needed a new idea and one that would involve Mike Jones at the outset but did not involve overseas travel. Then I had it. We would market specially prepared pet food individually designed for each pet. At that time you had dog, cat and fish foods but no especially designed pet food for the other little household pets – they were usually fed scraps that you knew they could eat. I got Mike Jones to design Gerbil, Rabbit, Hamster, Guinea Pig, Ferret, Tortoise and Chameleon/Lizard feed supplements to be sold in little individually designed packs giving all the nutrition and beneficial information on the outside. As with our other feeds these were to be added to the normal diet their pets were enjoying. Mike Lovett-Williams loved the idea and couldn't wait to get started. The company was to be called Bas Carbonit. Mike Jones, riddled with guilt over his wasted trip was only too happy to oblige as a way of making amends. I agreed to go over to Reading at least once or twice a week to help launch it, but with everything else swimming around me I was losing my enthusiasm. Bringing Mike Jones into it made the profit split three ways. I underestimated all the preparation time that would be needed to get the thing ready for marketing. I had bankruptcy looming over me and a desire to be with my family. I could see that this enterprise would take me further away from them. Not only was it based in Reading but Mike Lovett-Williams now wanted more and more of my time. I decided to bow out before the project was ready to launch. Although it had been my idea, Mike Jones and Mike Lovett-Williams were prepared to devote their time to it so I gave Mike Lovatt-Williams my shares. I wanted nothing for them as it was too soon in the project to evaluate their worth. As it turned out the business became very successful and Mike Lovett-Williams earned a fortune from it.

CHAPTER 25

MANAGEMENT ON THE MOVE

The second enterprise involved an American franchise for 'Management on the Move'. It was a form of head hunting that my sister's husband had been successful in when they lived in America. A list of vacancies for top management was canvassed and then possible interested parties were cold-called to see if they were interested. I felt that such blatant discussion were awkward for all parties. My only refinement was firstly to recruit a team of housewives who could do the phone calls from home, and then to put the vacancies in a magazine and just get the girls to ask a prospective candidate if he or she would want to know more or if there was anything else they might be interested in. He or she would then be on the mailing list but as an exclusive client to the person who first made contact. The magazine then had a list of vacancies and an anonymous list of top management and personnel looking for change. The companies paid for their advert (at a low cost first but increased as it became successful) and the prospective candidate paid a percentage of their first month's salary agreed between the company and the client. The women were recruited for their charm and telephone manner and initially I went round to visit them to put them through their paces. I put some of my hard earned savings to get the initial magazine printed and this was then widely circulated in given areas. I repaid myself from the advertising revenue and the women were paid a large commission from the clients initial payment on every job secured. A few initial successes set the ball rolling but generosity to the workforce meant that there was little in it to me and I didn't want to be involved in the groundwork. So after the first three months, having got my money back I passed the whole business and concept over to Elizabeth Brown, one of the housewives but a real switched on go-getter whose enthusiasm I knew would make a success of the project. I had no contact with it after that.

CHAPTER 26

HOME LIFE CRISIS

For the first time the business failures started to impinge on my home life. The erratic income I had managed to make from my various activities had meant that I had not always been able to pay debts on time and despite trying to juggle the various demands and delay them with letters and phone calls I had not always been successful. We had the bailiffs call two or three times a day, on one occasion Jan and I had hidden behind the settee so that we couldn't be seen when they peered through the windows. Eventually, I paid everything off but those odd occasions had added to Jan's worry and she wished I would "get an ordinary job like other people". I finally felt as if everything I did was useless and decided to give up on everything. I had some money in the Bank Romance in Switzerland from the magazine sales in Czechoslovakia from a few years ago and I decided that I should fly out there to get it. I contacted Derek Parkhouse to organise and send me the paperwork and booked a flight. It was to be just a day trip to Zurich to draw out my share of the money. I flew out from Heathrow but when I arrived at the airport in Zurich they wouldn't let me in. My passport was out of date. The trouble was I wasn't aloud to fly back to London either as I didn't have a valid passport. I was stuck in limbo. After spending most of the day at the airport they eventually arranged through the Swiss Government a 'Visa Exceptionnel' on payment of a total of £80. But I still wasn't allowed into Switzerland, the document only allowed me to return to London, a very expensive and abortive day trip. I never went back for the money and now I was £80 worse off. Then just to crown it all the engine of my little sports car blew up one day on the way back from London on the motorway. I hadn't had it all that long and the garage said that the fault lay with the engine. What with having to be towed off the motorway and making my way back and then being told that the whole engine had to be rebuilt it was an expense I could do without. I took the matter up with Don Finlay who had made the car as I thought that he was partly to blame and should help share some of the cost but he totally refused and said that I hadn't taken care of it and had probably raced the engine (which I knew I hadn't). It would take almost six months before I got the car back.

CHAPTER 27

JAN COULDN'T PUT UP WITH IT ALL

It was all over. Jan told me that she "had enough and couldn't put up with our life-style anymore". I told Jan that, just like her, I couldn't put up with it anymore either and I was going to sign on and become unemployed. Before I did that however, I had one further thing to do. I needed to save the house from my inevitable bankruptcy. I arranged a paper sale to Jan's dad and then a repurchase back in Jan's name. I filled in the forms saying that Jan was employed by Alban ISO and got Mike Jones to verify a salary sufficient for the borrowing. Then the whole thing was done on a back to back basis so Jan's dad didn't have to find any money and the only costs were those of a local conveyancer who I had used, he had no knowledge of what it was all about. With the house safe I could relax. Mike Jones meanwhile went to live in Whitstable in Kent where his wife had bought a house from the money she had prudently kept from the sale of their house in Ashbourne. The next few months Jan always referred to as the happiest of her life. We spent every moment together, going for long walks or just being in the house together. Jan became pregnant in the April.

CHAPTER 28

MY SISTERS 2ND MARRIAGE/& WALES

In June we went to my sisters wedding. It was her second husband, Chris, who looked similar to Tom Jones (although Trisha insisted he was better looking!). The wedding was in Caxton Hall and the reception was in the Cavendish Hotel. Like her first wedding, it was a plush affair and Mark and Troy again behaved so well that we received many compliments from the guests. It took her a while to want to get married again, but knew she must make a decision if she wanted to have children. She actually acquired an instant family; Chris had custody of his two teenage children, Paul and Clare. By this time Trisha was an Airline Stewardess and able to get the children free flights to Disney World, The Vatican, to mention a few. They all got on well together and later Trisha made up for lost time by having twins.

***

In August we went on holiday to Wales in the borrowed Viva as Jan's mini needed a new exhaust. I had carried on visiting Welwyn Garden City Stores taking Jan and the children when I had to deliver one or two other items from his orders that Leon Morse had sent through me. We stayed in bed & breakfast in Portmadoc and Pwllheli. Although the weather wasn't as goods as our previous visit to Wales, we all thoroughly enjoyed ourselves although Jan found it uncomfortable on the beach in her pregnant state. Whilst on holiday I started to think about writing a novel. I was always an avid reader and I loved history especially the Dark Ages. It intrigued me – that period from when Rome withdrew from Britain until the various Germanic tribes took over, a period of nearly 200 years. I had read so much of that time including many of the early sources and I was to go on adding to my library of the period with many books, maps and original manuscripts. Consequently the novel I decided to write would follow a comfortable Roman family in Britain through four generations, roughly spanning the fifth century. I would write in longhand and use any spare idle moments. It became a sort of hobby over the next ten years. I started on that holiday with random jottings and slowly added to it over the years. Our neighbours, Don and Elsie had looked after Toby while we were away. Elsie said that he used to disappear during the day but at teatime she would just rattle the tin outside her door and he would come running back for his food and the curl up on his bed.

***

After the return from holiday Jan started getting a little concerned over her pregnancy. It seemed different from the others. A lot of the time the baby didn't seem to move and then it seemed to get in funny positions. At one time Jan was even worried that it might have two heads but when she went to the doctor he confirmed that everything was alright and that she wasn't to worry. Howeve much reassurance she got, she remained uneasy and was becoming sure that the baby was deformed. She had so much wanted a little girl. I told her not to worry and reminded her of what the doctor had said, she smiled and said that she was probably being silly but I could see that she wasn't really sure. During sunny days I used to enjoy watching Mark and Troy play with their friends outside and often they would play in the field at the back. Once when the farmer put cows in the field and they started to come over to where the boys were playing, they all hid under an upturned long bathtub while the cows milled around outside wondering what was making the noise underneath.

***

Eventually I got my little sports car back, but not for long. One cold rainy winter night on the 12th December I was coming back from London. I had been to a meeting with the solicitors as the bank had renewed their demand for repayment under my personal guarantee. I was weary of everything and with the death of Norman Shine I no longer had the money or the inclination to pursue our counterclaim. Mike Jones had moved to Whitstable and the bank could not now trace his whereabouts, he was quite content to leave it at that. I was hurrying to get home as Jan was now in the last stages of her labour and I hadn't really wanted to leave her. Since my unemployment we had become inseparable but she hadn't wanted to come with me to London because it would have meant collecting Mark and Troy from school early. All this was probably occupying my mind that winters night. It was about 6.30 pm and I had just come to the end of Kinsbourne Green lane where it met the main A6 road to Luton. Visibility was poor and it wasn't helped by a big lorry parked in the main road to the left making it impossible to see oncoming traffic from that side. I slowly edged forward peering round the lorry when it seemed as if from nowhere this huge truck struck the front of my car. Almost as a reaction I drew my feet back just in time as the fibreglass shell along with half the chassis was split from the car and was dragged up the road by the truck while I was left spinning around in the other half of the car. My legs were cut and grazed and I was in a state of shock but otherwise I was alright. The rain was pouring down and through the gloom I could see the other half of my car where it had been cast aside on the verge. The truck had disappeared. Near the corner was Frank Pratley's garage, so I climbed out the car and limped up the track to his workshop. Luckily he was still there with one of his mechanics. I explained what had happened and between them they collected the two bits of car while I limped home, arriving back sopping wet and with two bloody trouser legs. Jan was horrified and said that I should go to the hospital but once I had cleaned up the mess it didn't look so bad. Back with the family I could just shrug the incident off and help with the children as usual and read them their bedtime story. Tomorrow was another day and I would sort it all out then.

CHAPTER 29

SURPRISE BIRTH OF TWINS

In December Jan went to the doctors she was still worried about the baby. After listening and running the scan over her stomach he told her that it was a breach birth and they would have to try and manipulate it around, but try as they might they couldn't turn it. Eventually the doctor told her that she would have to go into Luton and Dunstable Hospital for the birth. Jan was upset as she had both Mark and Troy at home and she much preferred that. Anyway I had to take her into hospital on the 21st December, the baby was due and they wanted a last opportunity to see if they could avoid a breach birth, but without success. It was Christmas time at the hospital and everybody was preoccupied and having to cope with much of the staff away for Christmas. I was able to stay with Jan for most of the daytime while the children were at school but I left her to collect them and take them over to my Mum and Dads. The first night Jan was left alone and in the morning they decided to induce the birth, they really didn't want it hanging on over Christmas. That night, after taking the children to my mum and dad's I came back to spend the night with Jan as we thought the birth imminent. However at about 9 pm the nurses said that I might as well go home as nothing was going to happen that night. They would call me if anything changed and Jan was left alone in the ward. At about 10 o'clock Jan started getting labour pains which started coming more frequently. She rang for the nurse but was told not to worry as it would be some time yet. Half an hour later with no-one around, having been through it before, Jan knew the baby was on its way. She rang again for the nurse who came in grumpily saying that Jan was making a lot of fuss and that she should be patient. Jan protested that the baby was on its way but, as Jan was never one for making a lot of noise, the nurse said that she was being ridiculous but if it would calm her she would take a look. When she did she was amazed to see that a foot was already hanging out. Then everything went into overdrive and Jan was hurried down to the delivery room, panting heavily in the lift to avoid a birth there and then. In the delivery room the doctor had a load of students with him and he asked if Jan would mind if they stayed and watched. By that time Jan was passed caring. She told me afterwards that the birth was extremely well handled despite it being a forceps birth and she delivered a little baby boy, but when the doctor saw the baby, it was so small and weighed just four pounds three ounces, that he was puzzled. He then said that he thought that there might be another one up there and sure enough with the forceps and Jan's help another little boy was born, slightly larger than the first at just four and a half pounds. It was ten minutes to midnight – if the second baby had been born eleven minutes later the twins would have had separate birthdays. They were so small that they were rushed to the special unit and put in incubators. Nobody at all had previously had even the slightest inkling that this was possible. Jan was given a sedative and taken back to the ward where once again she was left alone. Nobody thought to phone me. Drugged up as she was she had a night of hallucinations, seeing people passing and looking at her through the outside windows even though she was on the sixth floor.

***

The hospital finally contacted me at 7 a.m., and shocked me by informing me that Jan had given birth to twins. I didn't really take it in, but immediately phoned Jan's mother and told her what the hospital had just announced, repeating parrot like what the nurse had said. It was only when Jan's mum bellowed down the phone that I wasn't to be so stupid and what did she really have, that it dawned on me – we had twins! Jan's mum said that I must have heard wrong or they had made a mistake – she would phone the hospital in the meantime. Next, I phoned my parents who were equally shocked but my mum said "Oh lovely, Mark and Troy have one each to protect".

***

I then rushed to the hospital to see Jan. She was tired and exhausted and still a little shocked. She had wanted one little girl and now we had two boys! Then I took Jan in a wheel chair down to the special unit where we could see them through the glass. The nurses held up each one in turn, but they looked so tiny, especially the first one and Jan turned to me and said I don't think that one will live - we'll have to prepare ourselves. I said that they looked like two skinned rabbits. Jan's next priority was to be home for Christmas, it was Christmas Eve and they had told her that she would have to stay in over Christmas, in those days you could be in hospital for anything up to a week after the birth, but Jan was adamant, she had two other young children at home and she must be with them for Christmas. I pleaded with the staff and went to see the doctor. Finally they consented on condition that she took great care of herself and at the slightest hint of trouble I was to phone and they would collect her. I was using Jan's little mini and I took her down in the wheel chair and on the way back Jan said that we would need something bigger now with four children. There was such confusion when we got back, my mum and dad brought Mark and Troy to us, and everyone was so excited. I phoned Jan's mum to let her know that we were back and she was all for coming over straight away, but I suggested that she leave it as planned until the morning because Jan was exhausted and I was going to put her to bed.

***

At 6 pm there was a knock on the door – it was the butcher with our turkey that we had ordered weeks before. I had forgotten all about it. He said that he thought we would want it for Christmas and was surprised that no-one had come to collect it. I told him what had happened and he was amazed. He warmly congratulated us and wished us a Merry Christmas. Jan and I had decided to call our two little babies Adam (he was the smallest one) and Simon. Both names had been on Jan's agenda for Troy until she let me have my way and to continue the pattern the middle names had to begin with 'D' so it was to be Adam Daniel and Simon Dominic.

***

Jan's mum cooked the Christmas dinner and over dinner she told us that she had decided to sell her house in London and buy a bungalow in Caddington, a village she knew from when we had lived at Markyate. It was not too far away and she was fed up of living in London with all its traffic dirt and noise. She said that it had gone downhill from when she was brought up there and now she wanted some clean fresh air and a garden to sit out in. She had made enquiries and there would be no trouble selling her house and for the price she could get a nice little semi-detached bungalow in Caddington and still have a little bit of money to spare. It seemed like a good idea to us all and she said that she would start looking in the New Year. It was a nice Christmas and we all realised it would be the last one with the four of us, next year we would have double the amount of children. News of Jan's shock of producing twins, spread around the estate and she was the topic of conversation in several of the houses. For a while it didn't really seem as if we had new babies as they were kept in the special care unit and we still had two children to concentrate on over the school holidays. We went to the hospital once a week to see them and feed them but the nurses had adopted them and it almost felt as if we were borrowing their babies for the day. They wouldn't really feel like ours until we got them home. In the meantime I had to get a bigger car as Jan's mini was too small for four children and all the paraphernalia that went with two babies. I went round to Frank Pratley's garage to see what I could do about the sports car. He showed me an old Daimler he had. It was an automatic with a sunshine roof and with nice leather upholstery. It looked all gleaming and shiny and he said I could have it for the remains of the sports car and an additional £100. I could certainly fit everyone in so we shook hands on the deal. After five weeks they said that Adam and Simon could come home and that's when the work really did start. Jan's mum helped for the first week and after that Jan & I worked out our routine between us. In the daytime Mark and Troy were at school and I helped Jan with making up the feeds during the day and feeding them during the night. The only trouble was they were not co-ordinated. They woke up at different times to be fed and they couldn't even dirty their nappies in unison. Consequently all through the night and daytime they needed our attention for something or other. Both Jan and I were like zombies. At the end of January we had decided that our family was big enough and we would not have anymore children. We would forget about the idea of a little girl and anyway with them coming out two at a time it was more than we could cope with. Consequently I made an appointment to have a vasectomy. It was not such a common thing in those days and my doctor had to counsel me to be sure I knew what I was doing, but I was adamant. So I drove into the clinic in St. Albans and after the snip had a rather uncomfortable drive back. I remember changing gear and stretching my leg forward was particularly unpleasant.

***

One really nice thing happened one day when I was away. All the women in the immediate neighbourhood decided to throw a baby shower party for Jan. The rumour had gone round how shocked we were and they could see by my transport (in such an estate that was always a marker) that things had gone downhill. Also I think that they had seen that I was out of work the previous months. Anyway Jan and the babies were invited round to one of the houses by Heather, the woman who had taken her under her wing, and there the house was crowded with the other wives in the neighbourhood, all wanting to look at Adam & Simon. There she was given a drink and they all produced presents for the children. Jan was overwhelmed. She couldn't believe it, she had always been shy and not mixed much and here was everyone being so kind. It really made her feel special.

CHAPTER 30

A NEW MEANS OF SUPPORT

Now having four children to support I needed to find a job quickly. This would mean leaving Jan to cope alone during the day but I said that I would take over the night shift, as whatever job I had it was bound to be easier than what Jan had to cope with during the day. I applied for two jobs; one with a firm Arcode that was the Romanian trade agency for chemicals where I would be doing much the same work as I had done for Czechoslovakia. The second job intrigued me as it was the managership of a new up-market wall covering shop to be opened by the Morris Group. I sent a condensed form of my CV and I received letters asking me to go for interviews for both. The first one presented no problem as I knew the work backwards and the pay and bonus schemes were good. The second one was different. I had to go before a committee of about four people including old Morris and his son Donald and the Company Secretary and Chris the co-ordinating manager of the Morris Group. This was a new departure for them as it was to be their first attempt at moving up market as prior to this they were a low cost wallpaper and paint chain of shops. I had prepared for the interview by reading up in the library and searching through Kelly's Trade Directories for exclusive fabrics and wall coverings. At the interview I didn't really worry about the outcome as I was confident that I had secured the Arcode job, so I let my flights of fancy and imagination run away. Their idea was to have the usual books of high street wall coverings and samples backed by stocks, but of the more expensive variety including fabric wall coverings which they considered very avant-garde. I suggest that as well as these they should include the more obscure ones and I rattled off a few names. I also said that I did not think that there would be a need to carry stocks and instead they should spend the money on a wider variety of suppliers books of all types including the very small design studios and both

continental and American suppliers. I said that my impression was that the sought of market they wanted to attract, the people would be prepared to wait for something really exclusive. I also said that they could save money by employing only one manager to co-ordinate the two shops which could be staffed by enthusiastic art graduates that would cost less to employ and that way the two shops would be run virtually as one outlet with two locations. My final suggestion was that they should offer a free interior design service to kick the shops off and a competent manager should be able to do this. I said that I was confident that I could, but any person they employed who could show a flair for colour co-ordination and design as well as some managerial ability would fill the bill. I could see Donald glowering at me. It had been his baby and his ideas that his Dad had bought into and here was I from nowhere trying to turn it all on its head and appearing a bit of a know-it-all. They made no comment on my ideas but thanked me for coming and said that I had given them a lot to think about. I walked away definitely thinking I had blown it. I must have come across as pushy and too cavalier and I could see that the son definitely didn't seem to like me, but I didn't care as I didn't really want their job of shop manager working under Donald or Chris's thumb. It didn't matter because the next day I got the offer of the job with Arcode with an immediate start on the following Monday. I was sorry to leave Jan alone during the day and I had really enjoyed just being with her during the nine months of my unemployment.
***

The post the next day brought a more unwelcome letter. It was an appointment for my bankruptcy hearing in twenty-eight days. The following week I started work at Arcode at Mincing Lane in the City of London. I was back just round the corner from where I started in Lombard Street sixteen years earlier and I was doing a job I had perfected eight years earlier. When I arrived home on the second day there was a letter waiting for me from Morris offering me the job and wanting to meet me again to discuss putting my ideas into practice. I didn't know what to do. The job with Arcode was safe with good pay and bonuses but the other job I could make far more exciting. When I mentioned it to Jan she said that couldn't I just stay with Arcode until we had built up a bit of money as a buffer. I thought that was a good idea but not quite the way she meant. I went to see them at Morris again and this time I was surprised to see that Donald Morris wasn't there. It was just the other three. Again I expanded on my ideas which I had roughly costed out for the interview which included a car for me to use to run the two shops, a wage structure for the four girls, a duplicate cost for the library of books and a pc sum for decking out the shops. I also included the wage I required for running the two shops and providing the design service. It was more than the wage they had originally offered but significantly less than the cost of two managers. They were enthusiastic and the Company Secretary said that he would take my costs and check them against his own. Chris was particularly complimentary and, nodding towards old Morris, said that I would be given a free hand and all they would need was a monthly report, to go with the turnover figures, of my activities. Then I broke the bad news to them. I said that, much as I wanted the job and would have loved to have worked with them, it seemed that I couldn't. My wife had just gone through a traumatic experience giving birth unexpectantly to twins and it had been a very difficult birth. Unfortunately my place had to be at her side until I felt that she would be well enough for me to leave her. Therefore with great regret I would have to decline their exceptional offer. I was heartbroken as to me it would have been my dream job. It was a gamble, but it paid off. They said that they fully understood my predicament but they were all convinced that I was the right man for the job and they would hold it open for me for a month or so. It was perfect. I had the chance to possibly get two bonus payments out of Arcode before I needed to leave them and step into this job. When I went back and told Jan she just shook her head and said "Why do you always have to complicate things".

After a month Chris rung up to ask if I had managed to sort things out as they were anxious to get going. At that time I was just negotiating a huge order for 100tons of Rutin for a client called Jim McVie, a broker in Los Angeles. The price of Petrochemicals was going through the roof thanks to the Arab cartel on crude oil and I had an advance order for Romanian Rutin at an extremely high price that would give me a big fat bonus. I was also doing well on other Petrochemicals and was loath to leave for another month. I explained to Chris that things were still difficult but that I would look into the possibility of getting a nurse so that I could start with them. Three weeks later at about 8.30 pm, as Jan and I were relaxing on the sofa after finally having got all the children to sleep, there was a knock at the door, Jan said that she was going to lay on the bed upstairs as she didn't want to meet anyone. As soon as she had gone I opened the front door. It was Chris and I could tell by the worried look on his face that it wasn't good news. I asked him in and he said that they couldn't hold the job open for me any longer. They were very sad as they loved my ideas but they were going to have to find someone else quickly. I said that it was really a pity as I had found someone to care for Jan but they couldn't start for another ten days. I said that it was very sad how things had worked out but I fully understood their position and I was only to grateful that they had hung on as long as they could, but they couldn't afford for my problems to hold them to ransom and I thanked him profusely for coming. But his face had brightened. He said "Does this mean you could start in ten days". I said that yes I could. He then shook me warmly by the hand and said "That's settled then, welcome aboard – I am so relieved." With that he turned on his heels and said that he must get back and he looked forward to seeing me in ten days time. Back at Arcode I handed in my notice saying that I had just been made bankrupt and lost everything and could not continue working after the following week. It was partly true. The day I had met with Morris I had gone to see the Receiver in the afternoon. The bankruptcy was a simple affair as I had only one creditor –

the bank and had no assets with the one exception of the Daimler which I had so foolishly bought in my name and it was registered as such. So once again I had lost a car. I secured the Rutin order before I left but I could not receive my commission bonus until after the goods had been delivered and paid for but they assured me that it would be sent on. I had accumulated a good bonus in the meantime and I asked them if, under the circumstances it could be paid to my wife. They agreed and said that they were very sorry to lose me but they quite understood and would waive their usual requirement of one months notice. At the end of the week I parted company with them with a nice fat cheque made out to Jan and my wage packet.
***

The two shops in Hampstead Village and Wigmore Street were to be named Wall Street and they both looked very swish all done out in shiny chrome and mirrors with a white tiled floor. I can't remember where the launch party was held, but in contrast to the shops it was a complete let down. Firstly it was in some non-descript hall lacking any character and design. Most of the space was taken up with covered trestle tables in a row on which were scattered a large assortment of wall paper and fabric books, but there was nothing original. It was mostly a combination of the vast Sanderson range which could be found almost anywhere and some books from Coles, while certainly more up-market, they were the ones everyone used when they wanted something a little more expensive. There were a few other books showing Hessian coverings but little else. There were no books from Today Interiors, Osborne and Little, Toynbee-Clarke, Turners Fabrics, Bob Mitchell from America and Petite Fleur from France, along with a host of others a rudimentary search through the libraries, the Design Centre and a few exclusive interior shops scattered around would have turned up. I was so disappointed. This was the launch to show what could be offered and they had missed the boat. It would have been far better to have waited until the full library of quality books could have been amassed. There were drinks available at the entrance

and the exhibition was opened by a totally bored Diana Rigg who walked round the table feigning interest with Donald and Morris in her train. Occasionally she would stop and flick through a book muttering "Very nice" but you could see that she was just going through the motions. The four girls who would help me run the shops and to whom I was introduced earlier were totally ignored and so was I. My other disappointment was the transport they gave me. It was a mini-van emblazoned with 'Wall Street' and the signpost logo all over it, hardly what I was hoping to take Jan and the four children around in. After the exhibition I suggested to the girls that we go for a drink to get to know each other and swap ideas. Sue and Louise would start in the Hampstead shop and Natalie and Anne would be in the Wigmore Street one. They were all nice girls and all ex-art students and we all got on well together. Natalie Giltsoff was especially talented as well as being a good deputy for me and she would later make her name in the design world. I told them of some of the books I thought we ought to get and they told me of several more I hadn't even heard of. They also said that, when they toured the shops they thought that they would be enhanced by a few minimal displays of sample pieces of wall papers and fabrics with the wow factor as they were too Spartan at the moment. They were full of ideas and I knew that we would work well together. I went back and told Jan of the fiasco of the exhibition but how enthusiastic I was about the girls I was working with. She was pleased but more pleased when I took over the chores with the children.
**

The next day I gave Chris a list of the books we needed and said that if he liked, the girls and I would phone round to introduce ourselves and order the books. He said that he would check with Donald Morris and get back. As expected he said that Donald Morris would phone the companies, introducing himself and order the books. As the library of what we could offer grew, so did the customers. We agreed that the girls would give advice on interior design in the shop and I would do home visits unless they were in the

evening when the senior girl Natalie said that she would do them for me and we would all consult the next day. It all worked like a dream. Our ideas of interior design would be to talk with the client to ascertain their taste and favourite colours and then design a theme around this using knowledge of what we could offer and pushing the boundaries of their taste as far as we could within their comfort zone. An example of how we worked was the request from a Mrs. Berman for something to liven up her son's bedroom come study. I visited her house in Edgware on my way home and inspected her son's room with his permission. My suggestion was to use a very striking large modern design wallpaper from Today Interiors but just to use one strip up the wall and across the ceiling and down the other side with the rest of the walls painted the background colour of the wallpaper so that only the striking motif was picked out, then to use the same design in fabric for the curtains and for the carpet to pick out one of the bold colours in the wallpaper. He loved it and Mrs. Berman was very happy. Another time I had to do up Jimmy Hill, the footballer's hallway in Bayswater. He was concerned about pipes being seen for the central heating he was having put in. I collected the pipes into artificial Greek columns against the wall and between the columns made panels of suede, painting the columns and the panel surrounds gleaming white to lighten up the whole effect. That went down well also. Another famous client was Alan Clarke of the Hollies who was redecorating his house in Belsize Park. He had very definite ideas of what he wanted and it was just a case of interpreting his wishes with our knowledge of the wallpaper and fabric designs we had. It was all great fun and sometimes I was able to take Jan with me on the house visits when her mother would look after the babies for a couple of hours.
***

Quite early on it was obvious that, with all the chrome, glass and white tiled floors we would need a cleaner and when I mentioned this after one of my visits with Jan back at her mother's house, Jan's mum said she would do it. I told Chris I had found a cleaner and then for two days a week I would bring Jan and the children up to her mothers early and then take her mother round to shops, running her back afterwards. She got on well with the girls as did Jan when she came into the shops and they adored the babies. The only trouble was cramming everyone into the minivan. It was the same when we went out at weekends. Jan and I would sit in the front and the babies would be in the back in their double detachable pram top sitting on the collapsed wheels with Adam & Simon alongside. One of the neighbours asked me if I was a magician, being able to fit so much into such a small space.

***

One day when I got to the Hampstead shop I could see Louise had been crying. I asked her what was the matter and she said everything. I told her to dry her eyes and come for a walk with me on Hampstead Heath and she could tell me all about it. We walked for ages while she spilled out her life story. She was a half-caste South African girl, very pretty and very emotional. I had noticed her enthusiasm and excitement with customers when talking about their designs. She didn't get on with her mother and she hated her mother's new boyfriend especially as he had tried to make improper advances to her. Now her mother was moving away and insisting that Louise went with her and her new boyfriend. They were going to live in Manchester and she hated and loathed the idea and said that she would rather be dead. In fact she had thought about doing away with herself, when she was younger she had gone through a spell of self-harming. I said that she was old enough now and if she really felt that strongly about it she didn't have to go. We would try to sort something out. I suggested that after work we all meet up with the other three girls and thrash something out between us. It was only then that I noticed that throughout the walk she had been holding my hand. She then flung her arms round me and gave me a great big kiss and said that she felt better already and she knew I would work something out to help her. The answer was easier than I expected. When we met after work Anne announced that Louise could move in with her and her flatmate. They had a spare room and Louise had already met the girl Anne shared with and they got on well. Then we all told Louise that she should stand up to her mother but if she couldn't I would give her time out in the day to go back with Anne to get her things and she should leave her mother a letter of explanation. Apparently it all worked out fine as Louise moved in with Anne and I never heard any more about it.

CHAPTER 31

FAMILY HOLIDAY IN DORSET

That summer Jan and I took Mark and Troy and our two new babies, Adam & Simon on holiday to West Bay in Dorset for a week. I hired the Datsun again as we couldn't all cram into the mini-van for that journey and my Mum and Dad followed as they were joining us for the weekend. We were staying in a flat on the top floor overlooking the beach and on Sunday night there was the most horrific storm. We watched from our top floor windows as waves came crashing over the sea wall and flooding into the street below. Benches were being uprooted and cars showered with gravel. Great arcs of lightning swept the sky and the thunder was deafening. Mark and Troy watched entranced whilst Adam and Simon wailed and screamed to match the thunder and lightning. Eventually the storm died down and we all got to bed. In the morning the scene outside looked like a battlefield. The shingle from the beach was all piled across the road making it totally impassable, fences were wrecked and the seats on the promenade had all been picked up and hurled across the road. The few cars parked along the front were all out of alignment and pebble dashed with the paintwork ruined. Luckily our cars were parked in the car park behind the block of flats and had been screened from the raging sea. That morning mum and dad went home and the weather brightened up which lasted for the rest of the week.
***

With the children we would all spend the day on the beach, having packed the feeds and nappies etc. for the babies and a packed lunch for Mark and Troy and ourselves. In the evening Jan would cook a meal in the flat while I looked after the children. One day we were on the beach at Lyme Regis. Jan and I were feeding the babies and Mark and Troy had been playing on the beach and paddling in the water. Suddenly Troy came running up and said that Mark was out in the water and was waving. He pointed to a little figure in the distance way out to sea, bobbing up and down and waving his arms and calling out. He seemed so far out and Jan and I were horrified. Neither of us could swim but without thinking I just ran out into the water fully dressed while Jan started shouting that's my son out there and my husband can't swim. I waded out as fast as I could but my sopping clothes made the way difficult. Eventually I reached the end of my depth and the water was up to my chin. Mark was still a good 50 yards further out. He wasn't panicking but he was waving and shouting call the coast guard and I noticed that he had his arm bands on. Their buoyancy must have carried him out but at least they were keeping him afloat. I started to tread water, pulling myself through the sea with my arms in desperation. Whenever I looked at him the distance seemed just as great and I could no longer feel any ground beneath my feet. Eventually I reached him and hugged him tight but now we had to try to get back and I really didn't know how. I remember thinking that if the worst came at least he wouldn't drown alone. I asked Mark to hold on to my shoulders and once again started pulling at the sea with both arms trying to propel myself forward. I could see Jan in the distance on the beach frantically waving and small a crowd had gathered to watch but nobody was coming out into the water to help. I cursed the fact that I always wanted to find the least crowded part of a beach. If I had stayed where the majority of people were someone there would surely have been a powerful enough swimmer to come and help. After what seemed like an eternity I suddenly felt ground under my feet. I could just touch it on tip toe and now I renewed my efforts and soon I was standing on the sea bed with the sea around my neck. It still seemed like hours before I was finally wading out of the sea with my clothes weighing me down. Just as I arrived at the shore a large woman in a bathing costume came up and said that someone had just asked her to help rescue us. I thanked her and said that we were alright now. Jan picked up Mark and in between hugs and kisses she scolded him for going into the sea like that with his arm bands and he had given us the fright of our lives. I was exhausted and still in a daze. We collected up all our things, Adam and Simon had been put in the pram, and we all left the beach in a state of shock. We had to walk through part of the town to get to where I had parked the car and I noticed people staring at our bedraggled group, especially me with my clothes ringing wet and puddles of water marking my progress. I drove back to the flat in my squelching clothes soaking the car seats, but I didn't seem to notice anything. Once back and changed I was able to run my mind over what had happened and how lucky we were that Troy had told us when he did. Five or ten minutes later and Mark would have certainly been way beyond my reach and by the time any help came he may have been lost for ever. The next morning when we woke up Jan could hardly move her arms; she had muscle strain from all that frantic waving. That was the last day of our holiday and we didn't fancy going to the beach so we drove into Dorchester and walked round the shops instead and then went to see Thomas Hardy's house in the woods.

CHAPTER 32

INTERIOR DESIGN BUSINESS

Towards the end of the year an Indian gentleman came into the shop in Wigmore Street. He owned an Indian antique shop in 21 Barrett Street just off Oxford Street, London, and he had just bought a house in Golders Green. He wanted to completely refurbish it and he wanted me to sort it all out for him. It was one of those meetings that were once again to alter the shape of my life although I didn't realise it then. Natalie had left the Wigmore Street shop in September to concentrate on her own designs and she had been replaced by Jackie, an art school friend of Sue's. She was cheeky and sassy but we hit it of straight away with the same sense of humour and she knew her stuff. Meanwhile I contacted Natalie to design some particular wall covering Narang wanted that depicted one of the Indian Temple paintings. Narang provided me with a photo which I sent her and I told him that it would take a few weeks to work out. He said that he would be away for a few weeks and would contact us when he got back. Shortly after that I was summoned to Morris Head Office for a meeting. Both shops had been doing exceptionally well and business was booming so I assumed that I would be going there to be congratulated on how everything was working. I couldn't have been more wrong. When I got there I was summoned into Morris's office. There behind the big desk sat the old man and his son Donald. The expression on the old man's face looked slightly sheepish while Donald looked very smug with a slight leer on his face. The old man started off by saying how pleased they were that everything was going so well and it had more than justified the confidence he had shown in Donald's idea when it was first put to him. But now was the time for a rationalisation of the business and Donald wanted to take a more hands on approach. To this effect Donald had decided that he was going to run the Wigmore Street shop himself and oversee the whole enterprise although I would continue as manager of the

Hampstead shop but answerable to Donald. Furthermore Donald had decided that we should dispense with the free interior design service as it had served its purpose but made no money for the company and was a drain on its manpower resources. I said that I thought they misread the free interior design service as far from being a drain it actually often brought more business in. In many cases the advice we had been able to give led to more than the original room being refurbished in the home. I also said that I had nothing against Donald but that I had been used to being more or less my own boss and consequently I felt that it would be better if I handed in my resignation. Donald Morris couldn't hide the delight on his face but he said that he was very sorry that I felt the way I did and they would be sorry to lose me. However as the new regime was to start immediately, perhaps it would be better if I left after a week although they would give me the full month's money. Chris would look after the Hampstead shop until they found my replacement. I shook their hands and said that it had been a pleasure working for them. Then I went back to see the girls. I phoned Sue and Louise and suggested that they close the shop for an hour and come down to Wigmore Street as I wanted to talk to them all together. Once we had all convened at Wigmore Street I told them what had happened. Their immediate response was unanimous, they all said that they wanted to resign with me and they didn't care they would rather be without work than work with Donald. Then Jackie said "Anyway Ronnie I know you. You will have something up your sleeve and we'd rather work with you even if it meant missing out on a wage until it all got going." I thanked them all but said everything had come as such a surprise to me but I didn't want them to give up their jobs. They could be much more useful to me for the time being in the shops. I had some ideas and I was going to see if I could make the interior design business work, but I needed them to refer to me any enquiries they got from anyone coming into the shops. I would work out a way of earning commission on the work I would do. We would all remain in contact and once I was on my feet we would all work something out together. They all gave me lots of hugs and kisses and said how much they would miss me but I could rely on them to make sure I got as much business as they could give. I thanked them profusely and said that we had all better get back to work now as I still had a week to go and if they found out that I had closed the Hampstead shop there would be all hell to pay.

***

During the following week I began to wonder whether I had been too hasty. I had a wife and four children, a mortgage and the bills to pay and I was a bankrupt without any savings, on top of which I had just lost my only source of regular income. Added to that I had lost the only means of transport that I could fit all the family in and unless I could get a decent sized car we were all housebound. That weekly wage packet with only domestic demands on it had been a novel experience added to which the petrol account had been invaluable. I had no clear plan of what to do next and Christmas was just a few weeks away and that would exhaust the months salary I had just received. As a bankrupt I had no bank account and consequently no access to a bank loan. So I couldn't even afford to fund the few ideas swimming around in my head. Still I decided that we would get Christmas over first and then I would have to work out what to do in the New Year even if it meant finding another job and working for someone else again, a prospect I didn't relish. As regards the car, my father came to the rescue; he offered to lend me the money to buy a cheap car. On the 14th December I bought an Opel Rekord for £575 lent to me by my father. On the 19th December I crashed an Opel Rekord coming back from collecting the car up from the garage in St. Albans were I had taken it to have the heater fixed (part of the purchase agreement). I was driving back along Kinsbourne Green Lane, probably with my mind in the usual whirl. It was at twenty past one in the afternoon of a cold December day and, although it wasn't raining the roads were wet. I passed over the motorway and entered the bend where the road narrowed and suddenly I saw a Jaguar coming towards me. I tried to swerve and brake but it was too late, I hit the car full force on the offside wing and was propelled forward into the steering wheel breaking my nose and spraining my wrist. Apart from the damage to the wing on his car the other driver was unscathed. I heard him shout at me "that was a bloody silly thing to do" and in my daze I got out of the car with blood running down me from my nose. I gave him my insurance details and was just getting back into my car when a policeman on a motorbike came up. I was still dazed and not taking it all in while the other chap was telling the policeman all about it. I said that I needed to get home and the policeman said that he would call on me for a statement. Luckily the car was still driveable and when I got back Jan insisted I went to the local hospital as my nose was still streaming and I was covered in blood. They washed my face and confirmed that I had broken my nose. They also strapped up my sprained wrist and asked if I felt I was alright to go home and I assured them I was. The next day the policeman arrived at the house with a summons for driving without due care and attention and without reasonable consideration for other road users. He then took a full statement from me and they dropped the charge of driving in a dangerous manner. However I was going to start off the New Year with a heavy fine and a garage repair bill to add to all my other troubles. After the policeman had gone Jan just said "I don't know – what am I going to do with you!"

CHAPTER 33

CHRISTMAS/JAN WAS OVERWHELMED

Christmas was spent as usual with Jan's parents although we could not see mine. In November my sister had also given birth to twins, but unlike mine they were not identical, in fact they didn't even look like brothers, and she had known from the first that she was having twins. My parents now spent much of their time at her house in Loose Valley, Kent as was to be expected, because my sister was also running the village store, and needed all the help she could get. Apart from this she was a step-mum now for two teenagers. Both good kids and she loved them, she would joke that she had teenage heartache along with teething problems to cope with now. So that's where they were spending Christmas. However, that was to be the pattern for all the following years and Jan felt our children were missing them, now suddenly they had disappeared. As the months wore on Jan became more and more upset, rightly or wrongly, she felt that we had been forgotten, as Mum and Dad were totally involved at Loose Valley with Trisha and her new family of four. On top of this Jan had been feeling run down with all the work of looking after four little children, she was depressed, and although she loved Adam and Simon, she regretted never having a little girl. This was especially poignant when our next door neighbour, who already had two boys Mark and Troy's age, gave birth to a little girl eight months after Adam and Simon were borne. One particular time I remember distinctly, in the early days when I had been working at Wall Street for little over a month, going home to find an exhausted Jan and she had been crying. Mark and Troy were on their Easter break and were running around at home and both Adam and Simon had tummy upsets with diarrhoea causing a constant change of nappies and clothes. As I came in she took me to one side and said that she had been thinking seriously and that there were a lot of couples out there who couldn't have children and they would love to have two little boys. She went on to say, she was lucky enough to already have two boys and perhaps we could think about having Simon and Adam adopted. She was serious; she was at her wits, end and felt that she could no longer cope. Jan's trouble was that she always had to keep the house as immaculate as possible however much it wore her out doing it. The children had a playroom and as soon as they had finished playing everything was tucked away in it and Jan was constantly going round wiping finger marks off and clearing up after everybody. Anyway, realizing how distraught she was, and I gave her a big hug and held her tight. I just said that was something we could talk about as soon as we had time, and perhaps tomorrow I would take them all up to London to see her mum and then I would wangle the afternoon off and we could go round the park, I realized she needed some time to relax, then after that, it would be the weekend and we could do some fun things all together. In her heart Jan loved the babies so much, but at that moment she had felt totally inadequate. The subject never occurred again and Adam and Simon turned out to be wonderful little boys; and we counted our blessings, as we did with Mark and Troy.

CHAPTER 34

A NEW ENTERPRISE

Just after the New Year I had a phone call from Jackie saying that Narang had been in and, although Jackie had told him I didn't work for Wall Street anymore he insisted on seeing me. I went up to see him the next day in his Barrett Street shop and he asked me what was happening with the picture Natalie was adapting for wallpaper. He explained that he now wanted that for one of his bathrooms and really would like it on tiles, but he was worried as the bathroom was small and he thought it might be too much as he needed the illusion of space. In the trade magazines I had noticed a new mirror tile being developed by Mirage Tiles and I suggested to Narang that we could transpose his picture on to a series of mirror tiles making up the composite whole but with the mirror background it would create the illusion he wanted. Narang loved the idea and he then said that he had a proposition for me. He wanted me to take charge of the renovations of his house and that he had great plans coming up for it and he would work with me to implement them. However it would be a few weeks before he was ready.

***

I popped in to see Jackie on the way back and she was talking to a large Egyptian gentleman in the shop. On seeing me she said here's the man I was talking about he will be able to help you. She then introduced me to the Egyptian who was a financier named Mr. Nagaty and he had an apartment in Portman Square, not far away. He asked me if I would accompany him to his flat and he would tell me precisely what he wanted. His chauffer was outside in a Bentley and he drove me round to the flat. It was very palatial inside, full of Oriental splendour, it looked perfect as it was but he took me to a large room at the rear which was completely bare. Turning to me he said he wanted the whole thing covered completely in mirror – all the walls and the ceiling. The only thing not to be mirrored was the floor. It seemed strange to me but he was the client and was definite. To clarify I asked him if he wanted the mirror to run floor to ceiling meeting up with the ceiling and cut out with a mirror backed door, leaving only the small window plain glass. I also suggested a mirror frame round the window. He said "Excellent you have precisely grasped what I require now tell me how much." I said that I would have to measure up and work out a quotation. I would need an up-front payment to cover the cost of the mirrors payable on a pro-forma from the supplier. The rest would be paid for on completion, but I had not come prepared and I did not have a tape measure. He called out into another room speaking to someone I couldn't see and came back with a tape, pencil and small notebook for me to work out the dimensions. It all fitted in perfectly. I could go to Mirage Tiles with a potential order for all the mirrors making sure that a commission for me was in their price and as the same time I would ask them whether they were capable of transposing a picture onto mirror tiles. If they could do it properly there might be another market opportunity. On the way back, chugging along in Jan's little mini I could see my new business venture mapped out before me. For bread and butter money I would contact the art collages with a proposition for students to design new wallpapers and fabrics on the basis that the best would form a new collection and they would get a royalty from every roll sold. The designs would be put in a book and Natalie would run off silk-screen samples. These with a selection of specially designed mirror tiles from Mirage Tiles would form the backbone of the business and, like Peacock Arts I would hold small widely advertised exhibitions to promote them. All of this would be funded by design work I would get from Narang, Nagaty and any others that came my way fed to me by the girls in Wall Street and hopefully after, by reputation. As the business grew I would recruit the girls from Wall Street to run the wallpaper, tiles and fabric side and possibly even open a shop somewhere. Then I remembered my Property Shop idea and thought that this would also be a step in that

direction but initially we were to be cutting edge design that people could find nowhere else. I arrived home full of my new project, although I only told Jan of the offer from Nagaty and Narang. She wasn't that enthusiastic she said "I hope you know what you are doing, you know what your like," and then with a rueful smile she added "Still I suppose you wouldn't be happy doing a normal job like the other normal people around here". I gave her a kiss and said that the way I was going to work we could spend more time together and she and the children could come with me sometimes and see what was going on and then we could all go out together. She just gave a big smile and said "We'll see."
***

I decided to call my new business 'Rechercher', a French word meaning to find or seek again, as I was really recreating in my own way what I had conceived for Wall Street. As a bankrupt it couldn't be a limited company as I couldn't hold a directorship, so it would just be a trading name. Next I had to arrange a meeting with Mirage Tiles in Northants. I explained to them my requirements for Narang and they were confident they could do it once they had a good scale drawing of the picture for the area it was to fit. The Nagaty order would be easier for them as it would be a series of large mirror panels with cut outs for the window and door. The panels would have to be in a manageable size and they recommended both adhesive and mirror screws for the fixing but they would require expert care. I asked them if they could recommend a firm to fit the mirrors and they gave me a name and number but said that, as far as they knew, the firm hadn't tackled anything quite so comprehensive. I then broached the subject of an agency for the mirror tile pictures and they said that if I could confirm both orders I could have it. We then discussed prices and after some haggling I left with what I thought would be very competitive quotes. I met the firm to fix the mirror walls at Nagaty's flat and they then gave me a price for the job. With my profit added I submitted it to Nagaty who accepted it. I was in business. After Natalie had liaised with Mirage Tiles I got a quote for Narang's bathroom wall which he also accepted, so the agency agreement could be sorted out. In the meantime I popped round to Wall Street's shop in Wigmore Street to see Jackie as they had another enquiry for me. When I got there Sue was now looking after that shop with Jackie. Donald Morris's hands-on running of the business had been short-lived and bad sales figures in the Morris Group had meant they were going to close the Hampstead shop. Ann was looking after it by herself with occasional help from Chris Maby and Louise had left to work for a design studio. All of the girls weren't happy and they recognised that their tenure at Wall Street was going to be short-lived. They were all looking for something else. So I told Sue and Jackie about my idea for the art collages and creating our own collection and they said that they would love to handle that and I could leave it with them. They would use their Wall Street connection to give them credibility with the contacts within the art school world. We agreed that we should try to get a collection together for the Décor International exhibition at Olympia in June where we could display the wall coverings, fabrics and mirror picture tiles. If all went well we could all capitalise on our new venture after that. I said that I would make the application immediately. Then Jackie gave me the details of an enquiry they had received in the shop from Irvine Sellars, the owner of a large chain of menswear shops. They had supplied him with wallpaper but he wanted help with some construction work. I contacted him and went to see him in his large Victorian house in Hamilton Terrace. He was an amiable little man and his house was being gutted for major refurbishment, but what he required from me was how to put into practice an idea he had for a swimming pool. He had already discussed matters with the planning authority and it had been included in the architectural drawings submitted but he needed to put flesh on the concept. He wanted it to be half in the house and half out in the garden, with a large glass wall to be lowered in winter to enable the garden portion of the pool to be drained leaving the remainder of the pool watertight in the house. I assured him it could be done and left wondering how on earth I could sort it out. I needed to consult a firm of structural engineers first.

***

Nagaty's room of mirrors was soon completed exactly as he wanted it, although to me it was a bit oppressive and when I took Jan round she felt the same. The firm I had used had done a quick, thorough and impressive job. Nagaty had paid up promptly and when I went to settle up with the owner of the business, Harry Manders – a robust hail and hearty type of fellow, I asked him if he knew a good firm of structural engineers and I told him about the swimming pool enquiry. He recommended a firm and said that, if I got the contract he would be very interested in doing the glass partition and he knew how to make it work and be watertight. From Nagaty I now had working capital and enough for household expenses for a couple of months. I met with the structural engineers Harry had recommended and outlined what was needed. After a site visit they said they could certainly do the job and gave me a price for doing the drawings and calculations required. They said that I would need a firm of ground workers for the excavation and tanking out the pool, builders for breaking open the wall, making the piers and placing girders to support the house and making good afterwards, carpenters for the partitions and shutter work, tilers and decorators, plumbers and electricians and lastly landscapers for making it all good afterwards. For an extra fee they would help me find the best people for the job. They would build this into their quote and give me an overall idea of what I could expect the whole project to cost although it would only be an indication as for a job like this with so many unknown factors it would be impossible for anyone to give a firm quote. A week later they gave me their costs and a ball park figure for the whole scheme with the proviso that it could well cost more if difficulties were encountered. Armed with this I went to see Irvine Sellars and to my amazement he agreed to give me the contract. I went back to see the consulting engineers and they were delighted. We worked out a payment schedule and soon had a team put together. Once work started and with the structural engineers overseeing the work there was little for me to do apart from my weekly visits and interim payment invoices. I would become more involved on the finishing.

***

Another lead they gave me from the shop was a Mr. Merkel who had just bought a luxurious flat overlooking Regents Park. Sue asked me if I could meet her at the address just to go through the wall coverings they had suggested and to find someone to do the work. Also he wanted a small balcony tiled. The wall coverings were mostly fabric, with suede, some Hessian flock and a metallic flock in the dining room - the overall effect was a sort of 'Jewish Renaissance'. I contacted Harry Manders to ask if he had anyone to spare but he said that he could only get me on old chap who was semi-retired but a superb decorator. The only trouble was he would need someone to work with him and he really couldn't spare anyone. I told him that I would be quite happy to work alongside him as long as he explained exactly what he needed from me and Harry said that he would knock a third off the cost. I spent two weeks as old Alfred's labourer and I learnt so much that I should have paid him for lessons. He was an expert in dealing with such costly wall fabrics and showed me how to avoid any glue leaking through the seams by taking the strokes down to the bottom, how to make sure that the duster for smoothing out was scrupulously clean and how to trim and cut. He was a lovely old boy and I really enjoyed working with him and while we were decorating he would tell me about all the famous peoples' houses he had been in, mostly pre-war stars of stage and screen. When the work was completed Mr. Merkel was very pleased and asked me if I would like a car. I couldn't believe it and I said that I would love one. He told me to come round to the apartment tomorrow and he would give me the keys. I turned up eagerly the next day wondering what sort of car I would get and then he took me outside and showed me. It was a black old Ford Prefect that he had bought for the number plate

'Ann 21' which he wanted to transfer to the car he had bought his daughter for her 21st birthday. I hid disappointment and thanked him for it. The car, although an old banger wasn't in too bad a condition and started first time on the button so I drove it away, it would do me until I got the Opel back from the garage. A couple of days later, on my way back, I went to a garage to fill it up with petrol and when I came out I got in to drive but it just wouldn't start. I tried to bump start it but it was totally dead. I went back to the pay desk and explained what had happened and said that I would have to leave the car while I went to get help. In trying to bump start it I had moved it away from the pumps and it was now over the corner of the forecourt. Anyway I went off not knowing what to do so I caught a bus to the station and caught the train back home. When I walked in Jan was surprised to see me as she said she hadn't heard the car. I explained what had happened and she said it was my fault for bothering with an old banger like that – I could have at least arranged for the garage to give it a once over. I never did go back for that car and I never heard from anyone about it.

***

Meanwhile, Narang contacted me to let me know that he wanted to meet with me to discuss various proposals for his property in Golders Green. The first problem he wanted me to solve was gaining access to a large basement room from the outside. It was where he stored his Indian statues and carvings and it had a door and windows facing onto the outside so that wasn't the problem. But from the inside the doors and windows were covered by a thick wall-to-wall curtain so that nobody could look in. What he wanted was to be able to stand outside his door and open the curtains before he opened the door to go in. Nowadays with remote control so prevalent that wouldn't pose a problem but back in 1975 it did, it wasn't available then. Anyway after some research I got in touch with a model aircraft maker to adept a model aircraft engine with its radio controlled remote to open the curtains. Narang was so thrilled with the device that he wanted another one to control a huge carved sliding panel door he was having made to go between the entrance hall and the lounge. The weight of the door caused several problems before it was finally accepted. With these two projects under my belt he started to let his imagination run riot. Before long I was designing a patio area outside his large dining room opening onto a swimming pool with an underground theatre on the other side with a wall of windows looking out under the waters of the swimming pool and accessed by a passage from the basement. Above the theatre was to be a large paved area with steps down to the lawn, flowerbeds and bushes. Around the perimeter of the garden was to be a large wall with alcoves at regular intervals to fit his Indian statues, each alcove lit by a spotlight all controlled from a power box in the kitchen. Then he wanted a small switch hidden behind one of the statues with another in the kitchen control box that would activate a small square portion of the paved area above the theatre and lower it down into the theatre below. This was to prove a nightmare of hydraulics but using the consulting engineers that I had for Sellar's property it was finally solved. The only problem was that planning regulations insisted that we had a protective fence around the top of the lift area to be lowered which spoilt the whole effect. Narang's solution was simple. We put the fence up for the inspection, then remove it afterwards and make good the paving around so that no-one would know where the lift was until he started to lower it. His next idea was where I made my first big mistake. He wanted a glass bridge from the dining room patio over the swimming pool to the paved area on the far side. I used special toughened Lexan glass with a tanalised silvered steel frame and the balustrade along the patio continuing over the bridge. The effect was beautiful, especially with the sun or moonlight glinting on the glass and water. The only trouble was when the bridge was wet it was impossible to stand on it and the graceful arch made it worse, once on it you slid in every direction and you could only gross it by crawling on your belly and pulling yourself along by the balustrade. It was a case of trying to work it out again, although the money wasted never seemed to bother Narang. On one occasion I had wallpapered a room in an extremely expensive fabric wallcovering from Bob Mitchell of Santa Monica in California. It was a dark brown flock pattern on a light brown Hessian and cost £180 for an eight yard roll. It had been chosen by Narang for the room where I had put a spiral staircase leading to the roof garden. It had only just been finished when his older brother came round and said that he didn't like it and ordered me to emulsion over it with cream emulsion.

***

As I said the cost always seemed to have no bearing on what they wished to do. It was impossible to give quotations for the work especially as Narang was constantly changing his mind or adding things so we developed a system. Every fortnight I would go to Narang's Shop in Barrett Street with an invoice for all the labour and materials used during the previous week plus my 10% management fee and then I had to undergo about an hour of arguing and bargaining while he tried to knock the cost down and he wouldn't be satisfied until he had knocked about 15% off of my bills. After the first month I realised that I had to add 15% to all my prices before I submitted them, it was a sort of game to him. Then he would get out an attaché case with a combination lock and when it was opened it was completely full of bundles of £20 notes. He would then take out as much as was needed to cover my invoice and any sum under £20 was made up by his secretary, Usha, with cash from the till. Once when I was waiting for Narang, Usha told me how he came to buy the house in Golders Green. Apparently he was at a party there when he told the host that he loved the house and if ever he wanted to sell it to let him know and he would pay cash, he only had to name his price. Anyway the host told another of his guests, who happened to be in property and asked him what he thought the house was worth. Having been told the price, he then asked Narang if he could have a word. He told him that he had been thinking about moving for some time and if Narang was serious he was prepared to offer the

house to him. He then doubled the price he had been told the house was worth and said that he would be prepared to accept a cash offer for that. Narang shook hands on the deal said that he would pay the price asked in cash on condition that the completion was done in one month and so it happened. The house was at the bottom of a cul-de-sac but not overlooked by any other property, with a long garden backing onto the North Circular Road. Narang also had a an expensive flat in the Watergardens, Bayswater and the family home where his brother lived was in Bishops Avenue, Hampstead, known locally as Millionaires Row. I was invited for a meal once at the Watergardens where I sat round the table with Narang, his wife, two children and about four other people. The food was brought to the table by what appeared to be staff and was a delicious mix of delicately flavoured curries. There was no cutlery, just finger bowls and serviettes, but what intrigued me was a pulley system over the tables on which hung the wine bottles. You just seemed to have some contraption for winding the bottle towards you and you then held up your glass and tilted the bottle. It seemed extremely labour intensive for just a simple operation.
***

In June we had the Décor International exhibition and our Rechercher stand. Sue and Jackie and with Anne's help had done a wonderful job of organising promising art students with their designs and between them had already printed some which had been sold prior to the exhibition. I had used one of the designs in Narang's house for one of his rooms, but I think that was one of Sue and Jackie's own compilations. Natalie also had a solid contribution with her wonderful fabric designs and her range of ceramic tiles as well as her exclusive picture mirror tiles for Mirage who also gave us a lot of additional display material. I helped with the stand but it was really the girls that made it look so outstanding and I also helped man the stand. Sue and Jackie were using their holiday from Wall Street to organise and run the exhibition in the hope that if it was successful they could hand in their notices. Natalie was already freelance and running a successful little design business as well as being an avid collector of buttons that she bought and sold at antique fairs. While we were setting up the stand Jackie introduced me to two of her friends who were looking to start a business in greeting card and wrapping paper design and they asked if it would be alright to have some of their samples on our stand. Like Jackie and Sue it was just a tentative first step to see if the customers were there.

***

I felt guilty as I had been so absorbed in the work I had been doing for Irvine Sellars, and more lately Narang who was becoming a full time job, that I had given the girls little time in their endeavours. Consequently when the exhibition was a huge success with the girls inundated with enquiries I felt a bit of a fraud at being part of this success. Also if I was honest I enjoyed the challenges of the construction design work that I was now involved in that took all the hours I wanted to allot for work. I knew that if I was to play my part in the design business that had been the basis of the exhibition it would be eating into my personal time that I reserved for the family that was so important to me. So after the exhibition closed I took Jackie and Sue for a drink. There I told them that I was passing the whole concept and business to them and they would be entitled to all the profits. All I wanted them to do was to reimburse me for the cost of the exhibition but nothing else. They now had the foundation for a good business and I knew that they would be very successful at it. At first they protested, saying that it had been my ideas and initiative that had got it off the ground and they always felt that they would be working for me. But as I explained that was only the concept; it was what they had done with it that had made it a success. They were clever and astute enough to run their own business and they didn't need me. All I asked was that they gave me preferential treatment should I come to them to buy some of their fabrics and wallcoverings for my own interior design work as well as continuing to send me leads when they could and also that they get Natalie on some sort of contractual arrangement as a lot of her work complimented what they were doing. As regards the 'Rechercher' name they could keep that until such time as they chose to phase it out. We all parted amicably with lots of kisses and hugs and they said that they would always be grateful to me for giving them this start and they wouldn't forget me. Several months later they joined with the two girls that Jackie introduced me to with their paper and cards and developed a very good wallpaper and fabric collection that went from strength to strength. The company was called 'Paper Moon'

Chapter 35

I NEEDED TO COUNT MY BLESSINGS

Throughout all the confusion and mayhem of my business life, I have been blessed with a wonderful and exceptional family. Jan was a total perfectionist, to her the job of wife and mother, was something that she considered her total occupation and, for her satisfaction, she was going to do it to the very best of her talent and ability, and she did. I always knew how lucky I was. In my eyes she was beautiful, funny, caring, compassionate, warm and intelligent and on top of that a superb cook, what more can a man ask for? She was also very thrifty which for me was lucky, as I had a habit of going from rags to riches and back to rags again. She was a very private person, but in company she had such a natural way about her that people grew fond of her, they also loved her giggle and laughter which livened up any gathering.

***

Our four sons were turning into quite exceptional characters. All four of them were very intelligent from an early age and excelled in their schoolwork, but they all had such a wonderful and quirky sense of humour. Mark, from an early age, was a very clever mimic imitating all the people he came in contact with. I remember when he was less than two years old sitting in a chair in our bungalow at Markyate. It was late and Mark was always very difficult to get to bed and that night Mike Jones had come round to discuss various things. As Mike was talking, he was gesticulating with his hands one minute, then putting them behind his head or leaning forward and then back and crossing his legs. Throughout all this Mark was imitating every move and gesture. I noticed it first and nudged Jan. I was a little concerned that Mike might think it rude, but when he noticed the focus of our attention he burst out laughing. Mind you Mark could be embarrassing. I hated being disturbed by work when I was at home and one evening when the telephone rang I said to Jan "I bet that's

Mike Jones, he makes me sick, always worrying about something". Before I could get to it Mark had picked up the telephone and said "Who is it". On being told it was Mike Jones he said "My daddy said you make him sick" before I could snatch the phone from him. True words from a two and a half year old but embarrassing none the less; I think Mike saw the funny side but I'm not that sure. Mark was also a very shy boy when out in company he didn't know. At his first play school he stayed in the corner talking to no-one and when Jan collected him he was obviously unhappy. He didn't go to play school again until we moved to Harpenden and somebody recommended a 'Montessori' school with its accent on nature and one to one communication. Mark loved it and that gave him his abiding love of nature throughout his life. He hated public performances and when he was little, about four I think, at the Sunday school they went to, Mark had to read out a line of about a dozen words for the nativity. He worried about it all week and couldn't sleep. Jan said that if it was making him so unhappy that perhaps he shouldn't do it. But he insisted, he said that Mr. Fisher, who was one of the church elders, had asked him to do it and that it was very important. However on the day he delivered his lines perfectly. At primary school he was brilliant at writing stories and his teacher told us on visiting days that she couldn't wait to get Mark's essays back. For a little boy they showed a wonderful imagination and a breadth and scope way beyond his years. She would always take them back to read to her husband. He was also very good at spelling and Jan always remembers when she had to take him to the doctors when he was five years old and picking up a Dinosaur book to look at with him. Mark impressed everybody in the waiting room by spelling all the complicated Dinosaurs names. He seemed to be naturally clever at most things at school and a deep thinker but his only fault was his obstinacy. He would never do what you wanted when you wanted even as a little baby he would show off when you wanted to get him in the bath and once in he wanted to stay and would show off when you wanted to get him out. Then as a little boy he would always make sure he did things in his own time.

***

Troy, unlike Mark, was very outgoing as a little boy. He was very artistic at playschool and full of energy. He was also the least trouble out of the four of them, when he was tired he just took himself off to bed. Also he had an endearing quality of when he came back from playschool and later primary school, he wanted to tell you everything that happened and words would tumble out so fast he would stumble over them. Similarly if he was watching a program on television and Jan was in the kitchen he would keep running out to the kitchen to tell her what was going on – Jan would say "That's lovely but you're missing everything while you're telling me". In the Sunday school nativities and the Christmas plays at primary school he was always upfront playing a leading part. I remember the first Christmas play he was in. Jan and I were going to watch it when one of the other parents called out "Have you seen Troy – he's playing the Ringmaster and he's amazing." He always had his pictures on the walls when we went to the school and once when we were looking at one, a little girl next to us said to her mother "That's Troy's picture he's ever so clever". Troy was a real all-rounder; he was good at art, drama, sport and his school lessons. He was also a very popular boy at school. Troy did have a bad habit of wandering off sometimes when your attention was diverted. Once when we took them as little boys to the Science Museum both Mark and Troy were fascinated. However as we went from one exhibit to another we suddenly noticed Troy was missing. We searched all over for him and then we heard our names being announced over the tannoy asking us to report to reception and there was little Troy quite non-plussed. He had gone to one of the attendants and asked him to find his mummy and daddy. The attendant told us that we had a very bright lad. He was also very even tempered and as a toddler Jan only remembers him really showing off once when she was shopping in Wood Green. He was looking at the toys when Jan told him it was time to leave. He threw himself on the floor rolling around and screaming. Jan had never seen him behave like that before, but she just picked him up took him outside the shop until he calmed down. But all in all Troy was certainly the easiest to handle.

***

Adam and Simon were full of mischief from the start and as twins they always related to each other rather than Jan or I. They would giggle and egg each other on and were always on the go – little live bundles of energy. They were trouble from the start. I remember one night when I had persuaded Jan to let me take her out to dinner while her mother babysat. It took a lot of persuasion and Jan hated leaving the children and we rarely went out. This night was to be something special and Jan was all dressed up in her best clothes. Just before we were to leave Jan said that she would just pop up and make sure that they were all sound asleep. Mark and Troy were fast asleep and she quietly closed their door and opened the one to Adam and Simon's bedroom. They were so small they shared a cot and when she looked in they were standing up in their cot hanging onto the rails grinning at her. But what was worse they had both messed their nappies and taken them of and smeared the poo all over the walls, the cot covers and themselves. It was a horrible sight and bang went our chance of going out. Jan went to get changed and we spent the rest of the evening bathing them and washing down the walls and cot and dealing with their soiled nightclothes. It was a long time before I could persuade Jan to go out again. Our house in Harpenden was a large dormer bungalow and when Adam and Simon were coming up to two we put them in the front bedroom with the windows projecting out onto the roof and they each had their own beds. Jan and I were relaxing after the children had gone to bed and I had just finished reading Mark and Troy a story. Adam and Simon had been in bed some time as they went up before Mark and Troy. Suddenly the telephone rang and it was the neighbours from the house opposite. When I picked up the phone the first thing they said was "Do you know that your children are out on the roof." I nearly had a fit and I belted upstairs and it was true. Adam and Simon had taken all the bedding and pillows off their beds and piled them up under the window. Then somehow between them they had opened the window and were half out on the roof. Jan had followed me up and we grabbed and dragged them back in. After that we had to put locks on the window. But they always did such things in unison, such as the stair gate we had placed at the top of the stairs. Between them they had worked out that if they both pushed hard on the bottom they could tilt it up and crawl underneath. The first we knew of this trick was when they both came running into the living room giggling. Also they could be so wearing. For instance they loved to climb onto the dining room table (the downstairs layout was open plan lounge and dining room with a door off to the playroom and another to the kitchen) and as soon as Jan saw one of them on the table she would rush over and take him off and as she was putting one down the other would be climbing up onto it and so it would go on, despite her remonstrance's they would think it so funny and be giggling all the time. Also on a Sunday I loved to relax and watch my classic serial with Mark and Troy. We would put Adam and Simon in their playpen but throughout the program they would be making so much noise it would be difficult to follow what was going on.

***

When Mark and Troy were at home they would take a twin each and carry them around all over the place and always the same one, I think Mark had Adam and Troy had Simon. Troy was especially good with them, never getting tired but Mark used to sometimes get a little irritable with them. Still at least he was better than when Troy was a little baby and had first learnt to sit up. Mark would be toddling round and soon as he saw Troy sit up he would go over and push him down. I'm sure he thought he was like one of those little round bottomed clowns he had that when you push them over they bounce back up. Still as Adam and Simon got older they became such lovely little boys and so funny. Once Jan got over not having her little girl she never regretted her little twin boys. She said that she was blessed as she was with the two older ones. Mind I remember one other nasty scare we had with Adam and luckily it happened while I was at home. He was just a little toddler and he was playing with Simon when he fell over and bit through his tongue. It just poured with blood and we decided to take him to casualty in the small hospital in Harpenden. I always remember looking back in the mirror and seeing Adam in the back looking like something out of a horror film. All his face and hair were matted with blood, it had been bleeding profusely but obviously it wasn't causing him any pain as through all the blood he was grinning. The nurses rushed to collect him as we arrived and whisked him away. They cleaned him up and he had another small cut which they put a butterfly stitch on and somehow dealt with the cut tongue. Anyway he left looking fine and it caused him no more trouble. Still we will come back to all of them and their escapades later in this story. Also in June 1975 Jan's Mum and Dad sold their house in London and bought their little semi-detached bungalow in Caddington.

CHAPTER 36

THE NARANGS/TOO TRUSTING/ 1975 HOLIDAY

When I first started on Narang's place I was able to use much of the same workforce that I was using at Irvine Sellars house as the initial work was all structural but I did have need of painters and decorators and another carpenter to work on the inside. I was just mentioning this to the foreman when I went to see how they were getting on with Sellars' swimming pool, when one of the young labourers came over. He said that he couldn't help overhearing and he knew a really good carpenter who could be very useful to me and he also worked with a very good painter. I told him to contact them and suggest they see me at Narang's house preferably in the next couple of days when I would be there. The next day this young chap turned up. He was short with a black moustache and beard and long curly hair. He introduced himself as Ray Linseele and said that he was a qualified carpenter but could turn his hand to anything. He also said that he normally worked with another couple who were excellent painter and decorators. I said that I had a lot of work to be done in the house and took him round pointing out all the work I had on my list so far, knowing that with Narang there would be many more alterations and ideas to be implemented. I explained to him that, with a client like Narang it could be very frustrating. He said that he enjoyed the challenge and he would be grateful if I would give him a chance to prove himself. I suggested that I give him a week's trial and that he brought his two colleagues over in the morning. It all went amazingly well and Ray proved himself to be a good and versatile worker. He was obviously the boss and his two colleagues followed his instructions. It came that I could talk the work over with him and decide together the best way forward and I could confidently leave him to sort the internal work out while I concentrated on the construction stuff that was going on outside.

***

It turned out that Ray and his colleagues lived in a squat over near the Holloway Road. One evening when I had to go and pick Jan up from her mother's in Turnpike Lane I offered to give them a lift back. I was invited in and it was like entering a totally unfamiliar world. There seemed to be a lot of other people inside, both men and women, all young hippy types either teenagers or in their early twenties. They had knocked two houses into one with a great big jagged hole in the wall linking the two. It was squalid but reminiscent of the flower power hippy communes I had seen in San Francisco over seven years earlier. It was dark with dyed cloth hung over the windows and a mixture of woven fabrics and posters on the walls. On the floor were scattered home made rugs and curtains separated the various rooms and pervading it all there was a strong smell of incense with joss sticks burning in every room. They had somehow rigged up electricity but when I asked how, Ray just winked and the dim electric lighting was supplemented by candles. There was hardly any furniture but mattresses with coverlets over them and large cushions seemed to cover a lot of the floors. One of the girls asked me if I would like a cup of tea and when I said yes she explained that they have their tea black with honey. I said that would be fine and then I was invited to join a group of boys and girls sitting on the cushions and mattresses. They said that Ray had told them about me and it sounded like a really over-the-top house I was working on. Then one of the girls next to me asked if I was a capitalist and I said don't you need money to be one of those, Ray earns more than me. Then one of the blokes said "what do you do it for then?" and I said "The challenge" and another one said "you're still feeding off the capitalists". I replied that unless he had built the houses we were in, all by himself, so was he, Ray and his friends – all taking a capitalist wage. I added that the only way they could lecture me was if they camped out on common land and grew or raised everything they needed otherwise we were all using the capitalist system. While this was going on I was sipping my black honey flavoured tea out of a cracked mug and watching the inevitable joints being rolled. When the girl next to me offered me hers I declined and said I really must be going. I was invited to drop in any time and over the next few months I occasionally did, a couple of times when I picked Ray up in the morning when everybody was crashed out in bed and sometimes when I dropped him back after we finished early I would go in for more chats. The last time I did that I had been using Jan's mini for the day while my car was in for an MOT and service just before we were going off on holiday. When I came out someone had smashed the wing and headlight. I went back and told them what had happened and Ray said not to worry he would fix it and make it as good as new. Ray and I seemed to develop a friendship and I was putting quite a bit of trust in him on Narang's refurbishment. He suggested that if I leave Jan's mini with him while I was away he would repair it for me and respray the wing and I also asked him if he could act as my deputy while I was away and look after the work for me. The day before we were due to go away Jan followed me up in the mini and I left it with Ray. I also gave him £1,000 to cover wages and materials and said that we will sort out what he had spent when I get back but he would need to account for any money used. I went off relaxed feeling that everything was under control.

***

It was the beginning of September 1975 when Jan and I and the four children went on holiday to the New Forest. We had booked a little cottage down a little track in the middle of the woods. The setting was idyllic but the cottage was disgusting. The key had been put behind a loose brick in the wall and when we opened the front door the place was filthy and full of flies which swarmed around when we opened the door. Before we could unpack we had to turn around and go to the nearest shop to get fly killer and cleaning stuff and then we returned and set about making the place habitable. We all worked hard, Mark and Troy being given their allotted jobs which included taking it in turns to kill the flies. Even Adam and Simon got into the spirit going around with cloths and cleaning everything in sight. Soon we had it in a bearable condition, the carpet was still threadbare and the two settees full of lumps and bumps. We had found a vacuum cleaner in one of the cupboards and luckily the bedding was clean. Jan had made the bathroom as spotless as she could and between us the kitchen could just about past muster and anyway we reasoned that we would spend as little time as possible in the cottage using it only for sleeping in. If the weather stayed with us, it was bright and sunny when we arrived, we would pick up something for breakfast and eat it on the beach where we could spend all day and on others we could go for picnics in the wood.

***

We were lucky the weather did stay good and the one cloudy and overcast day we spent at the motor museum at Beaulieu and down to Bucklers Hard. A couple of days we walked in the woods and saw the deer and had a picnic but most other days it was very hot and we would drive down to Sandbanks and catch the ferry across to Studland Beach where the boys would play all day together. On the way over they would eat ice-creams in the car and Adam and Simon would be in their little swimming trunks and by the time we got to the beach they would be covered in ice-cream and then they would run on the sand and be coated in a sticky mixture of ice-cream and sand. Mark and Troy would then run them down to the sea and wash it all off. They all played so contentedly that one day a woman, who had been sitting behind us watching, came over and said that she had never seen such a close family and it was wonderful how they all got on so well together. She said that Jan must be a wonderful mother. It was while we were sitting on the beach that Jan and I talked about moving down to Cornwall where I had always wanted to live. Jan said that she didn't really like living on the estate as you always felt on show and she wished that we could work together on some little business like a shop or post office where we could be together all the time. I agreed and said

that as soon as I had finished Narang's job we would seriously look at the possibility of moving and if we had a shop we could perhaps sell wallpapers and things as well in Cornwall although if we had other things in the shop to supplement it like a post office or something it would mean we could have a regular wage. It was a lovely holiday despite the accommodation and even that had one advantage we didn't have to worry while we potty trained Adam and Simon. They went on holiday in nappies and returned without them – they were fully trained.
***

When we got back I felt refreshed and happy and it was with some reluctance I left the family on the Monday morning to go up to Golders Green. When I got there I was surprised that no-one seemed to be working in the house and when I went in it seemed that no work had been done since I left. I went out the back and asked the bricklayers building the wall whether they had seen anything of Ray and the other workmen in the house. They said that nobody had been there all week. I thought that I better go round to the squat and see why they hadn't been to do any work. I assumed that perhaps Ray had been working on Jan's car, but when I got there the first thing I saw was large notices outside the row of property saying that they were condemned and demolition would be starting at the beginning of October. I went up to the properties but they were all locked and boarded up with great padlocks and chains on the doors. In desperation I hammered on the door but I knew there would be no reply – they had all gone and so had Jan's mini and my £1,000. I waited a week but there was no contact so I had to get new workmen and this time I recruited them through a proper agency. I also had to report Jan's mini to the police, however they seemed to take little notice and said that I was a fool to be so trusting. The insurance company said that, as I had given away the car keys and the car to somebody, it didn't come under their terms of theft. Several months later I was driving down the Finchley Road when I saw what looked like Jan's car up a side street. I drove round to check and there it was by the side of the road with four flat tyres. It had a note on the windscreen requested the owner to remove it. I had an appointment but the next day I had to collected Mike Jones from the station, as he and his wife had made some curtains for Narang's property and I thought that I would bring a car pump and, if necessary a tow rope and we will get it home or to a garage. The next day I went back with Mike Jones but the car was gone and pinned to the nearest lamppost was a notice saying that it had been collected by the Council and taken away to be crushed. I phoned the Council and went to the scrap yard but I was too late it had already been crushed.

***

One day I decided to take the car down to my Dad's garage at the bottom of his garden as I knew he had a large rubber mallet and other tools I could possibly use to fix the boot. Mum and Dad were away at Trisha's but I knew where the garage key was kept and I suggested that Jan take the children to the park, just a couple of streets away and as soon as I fixed the boot I would join her there. It was a nice sunny day and the children would be better off on the swings and round-abouts. Anyway once she had gone I set about trying to straighten the boot out where the pointed end of the fence had pushed it in. I thought that if I climbed in the back I could lever it with my feet while I hit it with the mallet. Eventually I got it almost straight and I decided to see if it would close and I gently pulled the top down to see if it would meet the bottom, but I must have been a little heavy handed because the next thing I knew the boot snapped shut. It was now pitch black inside and I was hunched with little movement and what was worse I suffer from claustrophobia. I had to concentrate hard to stop myself going into a blind panic. I didn't know what to do. Jan was at the park waiting for me and it would be a very long time before she decided I wasn't coming and made her way back and I wasn't sure I could survive that long without going off my head. Mum and Dad were away and there was no-one in the house to hear me even if I banged and shouted and the neighbours were too far away. I struggled against panic to try and work out what to do. I tried to fiddle with the lock but it had snapped shut and probably needed a key to open it from the outside. Besides it was pitch dark and I couldn't see anything. I pushed and pushed against the bonnet lid but it wouldn't budge but as I braced myself I thought I felt some movement in the partition behind me. I braced myself and pushed hard against the back and I could feel it slightly give. With a superhuman effort I put all my strength to it and I heard the partition crack and I could see daylight at the top. Eventually after an eternity I managed to push the partition and the backseats forward just enough for me to crawl through and into the back of the car. It was a feat I doubt if I could have done without the fear and adrenaline rush that came with it and I had been trapped for almost two hours. I managed to get the seats back in place but the only trouble was that from that time onwards the car always stunk of exhaust or petrol fumes.

***

At the end of the year we had a quiet Christmas with just Jan and I and the children, going to see Jan's mum on Boxing Day. It was lovely just being together and the boys were excited with their presents. As usual we would put the sacks at the bottom of their beds and they would bring them through to our room to open them. Jan would cook the turkey overnight and we would all be up early and after breakfast, go for a walk before coming back and I would help Jan prepare the dinner while the boys played with their toys. Then after dinner we would play games before all curling up on the settee and watching television. This would set the pattern for our Christmas days to come. Jan and I rarely went out except for walks and once we had got the children to bed we would see the New Year in with champagne and chocolates.

CHAPTER 37

1976/PROGRESSING/ANOTHER SHOCK

I was back working at Narang's in the New Year as 1976 got underway. His work was becoming all consuming and I hadn't really had time to look for any other design work. I had replaced Ray Linseele and his colleagues with a more professional team and most of the construction work in the garden was coming to an end with the replacement bridge being the last job to complete with its anti-slip tiles made of wired glass. In the house we still had new bathrooms and a jacuzzi and sauna to build and some of the decoration to finish off and there was still the front of the house to complete. I reckoned that everything would be finished by late summer and then Jan and I could look at upping sticks and moving to Cornwall. The only problem to sort out was Jan's mum. She had only just moved to Caddington to be near her daughter so we reckoned that, when the time came, the only thing we could do was ask her to come with us. I wasn't quite so worried about my mum and dad as they were now talking about moving to Loose Valley, it was a beautiful 15th century village they loved and would be able to help out Trisha.

***

Then one Friday morning in April I turned up at Narang's shop in Barrett Street as usual to collect the cash for the men's wages and to pay the bills and I was surprised to see the shop shut and the window empty. The brothers had another shop in Cadogan Square where his older brother usually was, but when I got there that shop was closed too and the window empty. I was starting to get a little worried so I went round to Narang's flat in the Watergardens only to find that there was no-one there either. The most important thing was to pay the men as they relied on their wages to be paid every Friday fortnight, so I went to the bank and drew out all the money I had. It would just about cover the wages and the small amount of materials the men had bought which I always reimbursed with their money. I thought that perhaps the Narangs had gone away without telling me and that I would probably get a message from them, but just in case I hadn't heard anything by the end of the day I would have to tell the men not to come in on Monday until I had sorted it all out. I couldn't afford to pay them another weeks' wages as taking this money out had left me broke. However before that I would go round to Narang's older brother's house in Bishops Avenue and explain my predicament, I was sure that he would sort it out, but when I got there that was also shut up. There was nothing else for it I would have to lay the men off until it was sorted. I went back and gave them their money and explained that I hadn't been able to contact the Narangs and until I did I was going to have to ask them to place themselves on standby until it was sorted. It shouldn't take long but I would quite understand if they had to take other contracts in the interim.

***

Then the next morning came the horrible shock, Jan heard it first on the news while I was downstairs making her morning cup of tea. She had the radio on and she said that she was sure that she had heard something about some Indians being arrested and she was sure that the name 'Narang' was mentioned. In those days you didn't have the rolling news bulletins and the summaries before the main news were very sketchy affairs. Nothing was mentioned in the next summary so I decided to go out and see if there was anything in the papers. What I saw in a double page spread knocked my world sideways. The two brothers had been arrested for stripping statues and works of art from the temples in India and smuggling them overland into this country. There they had been selling individual items through the auction houses such as Sotheby's and Christies for sums of £100,000 or more. Apparently having then received the proceeds of sale they had nowhere to put them as their records could not account for a purchase. It had been taken out in cash hence the briefcases full of twenty pound notes or more and they had acquired a reputation for reckless gambling in the casinos. It was so much Monopoly money to them and they could not spend it fast enough. They had been extradited back to India where they would be dealt with very harshly for such sacrilege and all their property and assets had been sequestrated. So there was no hope of me ever getting my money and I had used the last reserves I had to pay everyone off. I was broke and it was time to think again and probably a good time to move to Cornwall.

***

The following Monday I went round to visit the entire workforce that had been with me at Narangs to explain the situation to them. They were all bitterly disappointed, it had been good money for them and they all had enjoyed working there. I had taken the newspaper article with me but most of them had already heard or read about it. There were no recriminations against me, rather to the contrary and they were all sympathetic especially when I told them I had been cleaned out. I had no right to expect anything else of course, but the only one out of pocket was me. When I got back home Jan said that I had visitors' coming that evening. I asked who and she told me, with a twinkle in her eye that they were Jehovah's Witnesses, they had called earlier and she had said that she was too busy, so they said that they would call back in the evening. That was all I needed, but Jan said with a giggle, that if anyone needed spiritual salvation, I did. When they called I invited them in, I was just in the mood for a theological discussion. They left two hours later and I never saw them again even after I had moved. Maybe my name had been put on some sort of blacklist.

***

I was anxious to turn my back on all the frustrations I had experienced and start a new life in Cornwall. I needed to try to forget all the various characters that had crossed my path and all the people I had been involved with. The only one who had ever given me financial support when I was desperate was Nick Nicholls who had lent me £3, 000 when I needed to save my house and transfer it to Jan. That covered the legal fees and stamp duty and I had repaid it back to him with my sincere thanks. He had volunteered the money without me asking for it and for that I was truly grateful. Others might have helped if I had asked them but I was too embarrassed and as the mistakes were mine I had only myself to blame. Now I was going to put my trust in the one person who had always been constant, Jan, although it would mean no more illusions of grandeur.

CHAPTER 38

CORNWALL

The first thing we had to do was break the news to Jan's mum and dad and see if they wanted to come with us on our new adventure. We owed that much to them as they had moved from London to be near us. They weren't too keen at first or at least Jan's mum wasn't, her dad seemed all for the idea. But eventually her mum came round although not very gracefully. I think she actually said "I'm not going to be stuck up here by myself!" So we put our houses on the market and organised holidays in Devon and Cornwall to look for a business and somewhere to live. Jan's mum and dad preferred Devon as it wasn't so far away and I preferred Cornwall, whereas Jan didn't mind anywhere as long as we were together and I wasn't spending my days in London. The initial idea was to look for a Post Office or shop that we could run together and a bungalow nearby for Jan's mum and dad. So our first week away was at Whitsun in North Devon at Little Torrington as a central place to tour all the businesses we had been given. We stayed in a little cottage down a country lane and divided our time between looking at possible places to live and work that the agents had given us and taking the children on the beach. We came across one stumbling block straight away as regards a Post Office. I was still an undischarged bankrupt and as such I couldn't hold a Post Office licence. It would have to be in Jan's name and she wasn't too keen on that. Also a couple we talked to in one of the shops we went to see asked us if we had any experience at running a shop. When we said we hadn't, the wife told us that we would have to be prepared to work long hours and we wouldn't have too much time for each other, she didn't know how Jan was going to manage with four children. She wasn't doing a very good job of selling the idea to us and we went back thinking that perhaps we ought to look at the whole thing more thoroughly. As regards the holiday, 1976 was the hottest year on record and the days on the beach were alright but the days travelling around in the car were hot and stuffy. Jan's mum opted out of coming with us after the first couple of visits and preferred to stay in the cottage garden.

***

When we got back from the holiday we hadn't seen anything that interested us but the agents told us that we did have a buyer for our house at the full asking price. It was the couple we had seen just before we went away who came from Oadby in Leicestershire and he was a bank manager. We needed to organise our second trip quickly and this time we chose a farm cottage at Alternun in Cornwall and my mum and dad were going to come with us. They had suddenly come round when they heard that we were moving to the West Country and, despite the fact we hadn't seen that much of them since Trisha had her twins, they said that they were very sorry that we were moving but they would like to see and help us if we were determined to go. The cottage was a converted barn opposite the owner's farm house called Trebullen and they had a large bouncy Old English sheepdog called Bullen who the children loved. He would come bouncing in and out of our cottage nearly knocking everyone flying with his owner, a very exuberant county type woman, in tow calling him to heel constantly. We organised our days much as before with one day on the beach at Crackington Haven and the next touring round looking at everything from shops, post offices to pig farms and holiday sites. The only trouble with my mum was that we always had to cut short our days on the beach or touring around as she wanted to get back to the barn to cook our meal as she said that dad liked his dinner on time. All the businesses had been a disappointment so we ended up just looking at houses as Jan and I decided that we would just get down to Cornwall and then sort out what we were going to do afterwards. We were getting fed up and then we came to St. Agnes. We had three houses to see there and I fell in love with the village. There was something about it that pulled at both Jan and me and we both felt that we could live there. One house was at Wheal Butson with a lot of barns and outbuildings which I thought that perhaps I could convert as a nice house for Jan's mum and dad. The second house was in Polberro and was a Georgian period gentleman's property and again had outhouses ripe for conversion. It reminded us of a property we had seen earlier in the week in Penryn which was of the same period and also called a Georgian period gentleman's house. It had a little cobbled yard with an outside toilet with two adjacent seats. The third was a newly built property at the top of Quay Road. It lacked character but was in a superb position with the school just up the road and the beach just down the road in the other direction. It also had the basic shops nearby and was adjacent to the cliff path. The house itself not only lacked character but was oddly proportioned and had a small workshop on the side. We couldn't make our mind up between the three and decided that the best bet would be to come down again with Jan's mum and dad to see if they had any preference. We had also found a bungalow that might suit them up in Lawrence Road on an estate near the village centre. Before we left we came back to St.Agnes with the idea of spending the day on the beach. It was a scorching hot day and all the car parks were so full they had opened a temporary one in a field at Wheal Friendly. We weren't used to the Cornish hills then and the footpath from the top down to the beach seemed steep. We were just settling on the beach when I realised in the confusion I had left the keys in the car. I ran all the way from the beach to the car park and back. I was fitter than I thought.

***

When we got back Jan's mum and dad told us that they also had somebody interested in buying their bungalow. It was now imperative that we found somewhere quickly and we decided to go straight back to St. Agnes and show Jan's mum and dad the three alternatives. We would drive down and stay in bed and breakfast and take pot luck. My mum and dad would look after the children. As I said before it was one of the hottest summers on record and when we got down there everywhere was full. We eventually found a place for Jan's mum and dad in what we later knew as 'Biggles' house at the top of Vicarage Road. Incidentally 'Biggles' had recently become notorious after a story in the 'News of the World'. He was a pilot and apparently he had been servicing an awful lot of the married women in the village. This coincided with another story of an affair between the local Doctor and the local solicitor's wife that had ended up in a cat-fight up and down the main street between the solicitor's wife and the doctor's wife. Anyway there didn't seem anywhere for Jan and I to stay. Then someone suggested we ask at the dentist opposite as he had done bed and breakfast once before. We went across and when we told them of our predicament they said we could have a bed for three nights. Jan's mum didn't like either the Wheal Butson House or the Polberro one as she said that they were both too far out. That just left Trevalsa for Jan and I and perhaps the bungalow in Lawrence Road for Jan's mum and dad, but again, after initially agreeing it, the next day Jan's mum said that having slept on it wasn't really suitable as there was that great big hill between her and Jan and the children. Meanwhile I had seen that an old shop opposite the Peterville on the corner of British Road was up for sale and I had suggested to Jan that we could use this as a wallcovering and fabric shop and resurrect the business I had been doing in London. We could work together and include the interior design business. As regards Jan's mum and dad I suggested that I could build an apartment on the side of Trevalsa, the house in Quay Road to accommodate them. We would start the building immediately we bought it and we could all muck in while it was being built. The extension would be built using their money from the sale of their bungalow and they would still have a sum left for themselves. Ownership of Trevalsa would be legally sorted with them owning a proportion equivalent to the money proportion of the overall cost of the property on completion. Jan's dad liked the idea and Jan's mum said that it was probably the only option if we had to insist on moving. When we discussed it Jan and I realised that neither of us were that keen on the house itself

although we loved the location and we could see that Jan's mum wasn't but we had just got fed up looking. So we decided that it would do until we got back on our feet when we could all look for something more suitable and the extension would increase the value anyway.
***
When we got home we put an offer in on Trevalsa which was accepted and the wheels were put in motion for the sale of our house in Harpenden and Jan's mum and dad's house in Caddington and the purchase of Trevalsa. The agreed completion date was to be 19th January 1977 allowing us our last Christmas in Harpenden and I was also to get a survey done on the shop we had seen. Trevalsa was going to cost us £25,000 to buy and we were selling our house in Harpenden for £24,500. Jan's parent's house was sold for £13,250 of which probably £10,000 would be needed to build the extension. I had already spoken with Clive Buckingham the original architect for Trevalsa and sent him my sketches for the development of the annex for Jan's Mum and Dad and he had already made enquiries with the Council and in principal they could see no objection to the 'granny flat' I was building on the side. I then asked him to start working up the drawings so that there would be the minimum of delay once we had completed. The only problem I had now was to ensure that the mortgage could be transferred and possibly increased to buy the shop which may be difficult as I was now an unemployed bankrupt and Jan had no job. Still with a little bit of manipulation I managed to organise another mortgage in Jan's name with £2,000 extra to pay the legal costs but I couldn't organise any extra to buy the shop so I said that we would have to rent one when we got to Cornwall.
***
Before moving to Cornwall we decided to spend the next few months visiting as many places as we could that would be difficult once we were so many miles away. Initially we concentrated on visiting East Anglia with visits to Aldeburgh and Snape, the home of the Maltings music

festivals. Then we went to Southwold and also explored the lost village of Dunwich, then down to Orford walking the paths around the RSPB centre and the River Stour and Flatford Mill. Inland we visited Lavenham and Bury St. Edmunds, Thetford Forest and Swaffham. They were mostly day trips and we would set off early with a picnic lunch and I would regale them with the historical significance of the places we were visiting, especially those centred around my love of the Dark Ages and Medieval Britain. The quiet solitude of the coast and the woods with their echoes of the past lent them an air of mystery while the old parts of the towns recreated a lost period. On some of the visits we would take all of the children, on others just Mark and Troy and I would weave the stories of the happenings in times past as we walked around. It was all an adventure and we all enjoyed ourselves. It reminded me of a walk I had taken Jan and Mark and Troy on one Sunday a few years earlier at West Wycombe. It was a quiet autumnal day and we had gone for a walk through the park and out onto the hills when we stumbled across the tower with a strange ball on top where the Hellfire Club met. I explained the story to them of the cruel cult the members of the club indulged in and we walked on and down the hill until we came to a cave entrance. There had been some work going on and there were electric cables running into the cave. We had approached it down a steep escarpment and not up the track leading to the front of the cave. Anyway I persuaded everyone that we go into the caves and explore them despite Jan's protests as I was sure that they were the caves where the notorious Hellfire club carried out their rituals. It was dark and spooky but as we wended our way down and round the corner we were startled by a dimly lit alcove in which stood the figure of a man in eighteen century costume with a lantern. It was as if we had seen a ghost but on inspection it was a waxwork model and as we plunged deeper into the caves we came across several others portraying various episodes in the Hellfire Clubs strange history. Then we came to the final chamber in which several figures were gathered around a stone slab with a prostrate figure in a white gown on it. It was eerily life like and Mark and Troy were both scared and excited and I could see Jan was a little nervous. There was nobody about and we made our way back through the labyrinth to the top and out into the daylight. We walked down the track and found a wire gate and fencing blocking our way out, so we had to retrace our steps and back the escarpment. Afterwards I drove round to find the track leading to the caves and the wire gate. There was a big notice on it saying trespassers will be prosecuted and another illustrated the forthcoming visitors attraction of the 'Notorious Hellfire Club's Secret Caves'. Finally in the November we spent several days taking Mark and Troy all round London visiting all the attractions including the Tower, the London Dungeons, Madame Tussaud's and many others.

***

Our last Christmas at Harpenden was spent quietly but we all enjoyed ourselves and after Christmas we got down to some serious packing. The owner of Trevalsa asked just before Christmas if we would like him to fill up the oil tank that served the Rayburn cooker and central heating so that we could have a warm house without having to bother as soon as we arrived. We thanked him and sent him a cheque as requested. The day of the move it poured with rain and down in Cornwall it was a howling gale. The removal lorry took our stuff down the night before as they were staying overnight and hopefully could make an early start unloading our furniture the next day. We stayed the night with my mum and dad and the children were going to spend a fortnight with them while we got the new house straight and then my mum and dad were going to bring them down and stay for a couple of weeks. Jan's mum and dad were going to follow us down in their car and their furniture was to follow on. As I said it was such a terrible day with the rain pouring and the wind howling. It was already getting dark when we arrived and to our surprise the removal lorry was still waiting in the drive to unload. The previous owners still hadn't moved all their stuff out and we couldn't get access until they did. They were ferrying their worldly possessions to their new house in a van going continually back and forth. We finally got access at seven o'clock at night and the removal men said that we would have to pay for them to stay over another night. When we finally went up to the house they had taken all the light bulbs and all the doors on the ground floor. We had to find the lamps we had packed away to be able to see anything. Everything was getting soaked as we took it up and finally when everything was in we were all so fed up and exhausted, we just made up beds on the mattresses and leaving everything until the morning we went to sleep. The next day we started to wonder what we had done and then just to make matters worse, when we went to light the Rayburn to cook breakfast and get some heat, we found that there was no oil in the tank. It was not a very auspicious start. Still it was a new beginning and I still felt that it was going to be a much better life for us all once we were organised. Things would eventually get better and we would come to love our life in Cornwall.

PART III: RICKETY LADDERS

Book Two of the Trilogy
More Snakes Than Ladders

R.D. Craze

TABLE OF CONTENTS:

CHAPTER 1 ....A NEW BEGINNING

CHAPTER 2 ....GETTING ORGANIISED

CHAPTER 3 ....HILARY AND MALCOLM

CHAPTER 4 ....THINKING BIG/DEBENHAMS

CHAPTER 5 ....INSPECTOR LEE CAME TO ARREST ME

CHAPTER 6 ....NOW TO GET ON WITH BUSINESS

CHAPTER 7 ....WE HAVE GONE TOO FAR

CHAPTER 8 ....A FAMILY CHRISTMAS

CHAPTER 9 ....FINDING STAFF FOR DEBENHAMS

CHAPTER 10 ....JAN WAS ENJOYING LIFE/I LEARNED MY LESSON

CHAPTER 11 ....JAN & I/TIME TO RECAPTURE ROMANCE

CHAPTER 12 ....IT'S COMPLICATED

CHAPTER 13 ....DEBENHAMS DEMANDING MORE ATTENTION/SO DID HILARY

CHAPTER 14 .... I GRABBED THE LADDER, BUT SNAKES WERE LOOMING

CHAPTER 15 .... ANOTHER OPPORTUNITY

CHAPTER 16 .... A MILLIONAIRE AT LAST?

CHAPTER 17 .... THE DREAM TURNED INTO A NIGHTMARE

CHAPTER 18 .... NOW TO RE-INVENT MYSELF

CHAPTER 1

A NEW BEGINNING

When Jan & I woke up the first morning in our new house and looked out at the view from our bedroom window, we couldn't believe our good fortune – it was as if we were looking at a beautiful oil painting composed from up in a tree-house. We looked down on the woods and across to the church and the village linked by the sharp escarpment of Stippy-Steppy with its picturesque old cottages leading steeply up to the village above. In the other direction we could see the fields surmounted by an old mine stacks and between that and the woods, a cluster of old cottages climbing their way up to the other side of the village – most of them with cement washed bow roofs. The faint winter sun glinted on the leaves, and the tree line silhouetted against pink strewn clouds. We felt privileged to look out on such a scene, and the chaos reining our house below, seemed worth it just to live here. We quickly washed, dressed, and decided to go for a walk before we started work. Jan's mum and dad still lay in bed so we quietly stole out. We could hear the river gurgle away in the valley below, and we took the path just a few steps away from the bottom of our drive leading to the cliff path. In all the years we lived there, the view along the valley opening out to the cove below always delighted us but never like it did with our first magical time, that morning. Far below the tide, rolled out and there wasn't a soul on the beach, and after the storm of the day before the air settled. We walked on and to the view looking down on Trevellas Porth, and up Jericho Valley and the pleasure of just being amongst all the beauty washed over us. Whatever may happen and whatever hardships we might face, we knew then, in such a beautiful environment, we could just revel in the marvels of nature and everything would fall back into perspective. That attitude slowly blessed our life, and in the years to come Jan and I would walk most of Cornwall discovering secret corners and beautiful vistas, losing ourselves in some of the most wonderful scenery to find anywhere. At first it would be just the weekends, following the habit we formed from our early married days, and we would take the children with us. As they grew up our walks became more frequent, and we would take a flask of tea and binoculars to find the most beautiful spot to sit and rest, drinking our tea and soaking in the surroundings. We always loved the solitude, and meeting people on our walks somehow took the magic away for us. We would walk in all weathers and with our waterproofs on, it could rain as hard as it liked, but best of all were those misty days when the countryside took on another-worldliness and you could conjure up the centuries past and the old myths almost came to life. We always enjoyed our togetherness, whether sitting in a field in the pouring rain drinking our tea or walking for miles through fields and valleys, across streams and up steep cliff paths with the wind and rain in our faces, or the sun beating down on us, both turned on by the beauty of it all. It was our very special world.

***

The first couple of weeks in our new house were a hive of activity, buying and hanging doors to replace the missing ones, putting up our chandeliers and light fittings, painting all the walls and cutting, laying and joining the carpets. Eventually we got it habitable and we put Jan's mum and dad's bed in the workshop temporarily, but it was imperative we got the plans drawn up and submitted for the extension immediately, as the present arrangement wasn't going to be convenient for any of us for very long. The architect, Clive Buckingham, originally built the house in 1974, and I spoke with him back in September 1976 when we exchanged contracts and worked out the plans between us. By October they went before the planning committee for approval, which was received prior to our completion. Clive was a very friendly affable person and reacted very amenably to our ideas for the extension. We then met him to complete the building regulations and he promised to deal with these straight away; true to his word, everything

was ready for submission within three weeks of our meeting.
***

Clive was a very keen railway enthusiast and like most enthusiasts he was especially fond of the old steam trains. St. Agnes lost its rail link in the Beeching cuts of 1962, and Clive with several others wanted to resurrect it as a steam link, as it ran through beautiful countryside from Truro to Newquay via Perranporth. It would make a lovely excursion from Truro to the seaside resorts and also provide a good link for the various scattered villages into the city centre. Many people subscribed to this venture with great interest, and eventually managed to put together just enough funds to buy the whole line with its stations and viaducts. However, when they approached British Rail they were informed that the price quoted did not include the track, and sadly, the final quote surpassed their reach. Consequently the whole project finally crumbled the year before we moved down, and British Rail swiftly set about dismantling the complete railway, selling off the land to local farmers, and the buildings to various enterprises. With many of the bridges now pulled down, the chance of resurrecting the railway disappeared forever. It was such a pity, as the route the railway took with its views across the countryside and coast with its link between the seaside resorts, villages and the city centre, were lost. What a mistaken decision, as now with various steam lines proving to be such tourist attractions, it would have been a money spinner, as well as preserving some of our heritage.
***

The St. Agnes of 1977 was far less sophisticated than it was to become, as was the whole of Cornwall, and it was completely self-sufficient. It seemed to consist of four main centres each with their own cluster of shops. At the top of the hill as you entered the village from the A30, the main artery into Cornwall, were the shops in Vicarage Road, with a garage, a stationers, a book shop, a newsagents, a chemists, a general store, a butchers, greengrocers and florists shop, a clothes shop, a café, a

restaurant, a shoe shop and a pub. Further down, as you approached the church there was an area called Churchtown and this had a post office, a hairdressers, an electrical shop, a do-it-yourself and general chandlery store, a greengrocers, two general stores with one of them veering towards a delicatessen, a fish and chip shop, a butchers, a bakers, a newsagents, an estate agents, a short-lived video shop, and another pub. Then past the church and down the hill you came to Peterville with its own cluster of shops and facilities. Here, some of the shops and restaurants weren't so permanent and often changed hands and function. The greengrocers converted to a print shop and a junk shop became a greengrocers, a general store and café developed into a surf shop, two restaurants – (one of them an up-market French restaurant), a garage, another general store and a pub. Our house was just a little way down the road leading to the beach and set high up with lovely views over the wooded valley and Stippy-Steppy, which was a terraced row of old cottages, climbing up a steep path to the village at the top of the hill, where there was a church and pub . The fourth centre was down the bottom of the road leading to the beach and this was the tourist and holiday Mecca with its two and sometimes three cafes and three gift shops, a pub, a picturesque restaurant overlooking the beach, and when we first arrived, a seal sanctuary. Also there was a school situated just a short way up the hill from Peterville. Very few of the major retail chains had ventured down to Cornwall. There was Tesco's, which was like a little local supermarket in Falmouth, as was the only Marks and Spencer's, Truro had two small supermarkets, and I think that the International stores were there, and they had two department stores, Dingles and Roberts, apart from Woolworths and Littlewoods, none of the other chains were represented. This was to be an important part when I later established my design shops'.
***

After two weeks of trying to get the house habitable, we were ready for my mum and dad to bring the children down. The house is on three levels, the lowest of which accessed by the entrance hall leading to the lounge and study. Then there were six steps up to the dining room and kitchen with a hall through to a shower room and a bathroom, with a further door through to the old workshop, which we intended to extend and convert into the flat for Jan's parents. A further six stairs led to the three bedrooms. Our new house was named 'Trevalsa' and we discovered that most of our neighbours had pretty house names, rather than numbers.

***

The ironmongers in the village seemed to supply everything we needed and were very helpful. The friendliness and element of trust greatly impressed me, which contrasted completely to the shops we grew accustomed to in Harpenden and St.Albans. For instance, when I needed some carpet tape the owner handed me a huge roll, and told me to use what I needed, bring it back he said, and I will just charge you for what you used. A caravan in the grounds came with our house, and my mum and dad stayed in it for a couple of weeks to help us with the children and chip in with some of the work. When they arrived the boys loved the house, spending the first few hours going in and out all the rooms and seeing what to discover in the garden.

***

The next day we were all up busy working again and in the afternoon Mark and Troy asked if they could go for a walk down to see the beach. Jan didn't really want them to go, but as the beach ran just a half mile walk down a straight road, (in those days children travelled short distances by themselves), I thought it would be fine. Jan finally agreed but told them they could go as long as they were very careful and didn't approach the water then came straight back. In the meantime we busied ourselves painting walls and laying carpets in the lounge and hallway, cleaning up everywhere and taking it in turns to keep Adam and Simon out of mischief, whilst my mum fiddled with the Rayburn cooker and prepared a roast dinner and fruit pudding. Then suddenly we noticed night falling, and Mark and Troy still weren't home. We really worried and cursed ourselves for letting them go off unsupervised. I started for the beach to fetch them, feeling sure they had just got carried away but just then the telephone rang and when I answered a lady said, "I have two little boys here whom I think belong to you." She said she lived at 'Tanglewood' just over the back in Wheal Kitty, and added perhaps I would like to collect them as they said they wanted to go home now. Jan and I jumped into the car and drove to 'Tanglewood', a bungalow set high on the cliffs overlooking the next beach at Trevellas. The old property sat in a wild overgrown garden with a donkey greeting us at the gate. A charming elderly lady answered the door and started straight away enthusing about Mark and Troy, saying what wonderful little boys they were, so polite and well-mannered and what delightful company they had been. She had told them that they could go back anytime they wanted. She fed them lemonade, cake, and biscuits, and showed them the donkey, her various cats, a small dog, and her budgie. When she asked them where they lived, they said they didn't really know as they only just arrived, but luckily Mark remembered our telephone number from their phone calls to us while staying with my mum and dad the past two weeks. Apparently, after going down to the beach and despite our instructions to the contrary, they decided to explore, climbing up the cliff and wandering around investigating the old mine ruins. After realizing they knew no way to get back, they knocked on the door of the first house they found, but no-one answered; so they then tried 'Tanglewood" next door and the lady asked them in. At the time neither Jan or I knew those cliffs were scattered with open mineshafts; if we had known this we would never have let them go, and to find this out at a later stage we were horrified, obviously there was a lot to learn, and this time we had been lucky. We told Adam and Simon how cross we were at their disobedience, and let them know we no longer trusted them to go out alone anymore.

CHAPTER 2

GETTING ORGANISED

Once the plans were approved, we wanted to make sure nothing delayed us and I decided to find a builder. I looked through the local paper, 'The West Briton', and contacted three advertising builders and sent them Clive's drawings. I had a rough idea of the cost, but I didn't really know the local labour rates. One builder quoted way over my own price indication, and although the second was quite close the third quoted the lowest. I decided to follow the third one, which came from a Malcolm Hill who lived in Truro. I decided to drive over and see him first, and then take him back to our house to better explain the details involved. Malcolm looked very much like George Harrison of the Beatles, although perhaps a little more rugged with a little bit of Dennis Locorierre of Dr. Hook thrown in, a young chap a couple of years younger than me and we hit it off straight away, I could see he was someone I could work with. A carpenter by trade, he toured me around his back garden to show me the extension he built for one of his neighbor's and I suggested, to minimize costs, I could work as his labourer on the footings, helping with the dig and mixing the cement etc. Afterwards, he could recruit what specialist labour he needed, but I would deal through him, and we would organise stage draws to coincide with the building inspections, which all seemed acceptable to him. I didn't know until later that his girlfriend, Hilary, was watching our meeting from the upstairs bedroom window, or that later Hilary would be influencing certain aspects of my life.
***
I then took him back to our house and showed him around, introducing him to Jan on the way through. I could see he was a ladies man the way he turned on the charm for Jan, and when I got back from dropping him off, Jan said "Wow what a dish!" She certainly seemed very taken with him. All seemed to go well and we agreed I

would call him as soon as the building regulation passed approval to start straight away.

***

One day Jan and I slipped away to do some shopping in Truro and on our way back through the village, I noticed the stationers in the square that did printing, and asked Jan if she might mind if I just quickly nipped in to see if I could print some cards and would only be five minutes. I parked the car down the hill and walked back to the stationers called 'Doodles'. There I met Doug Luke the proprietor and asked him about the cards I wanted for my design business. During our conversation I told him that I was looking for business premises, and thought about seeing if could rent a shop at the bottom of the hill. Doug surprised me then, by suggesting I could share his premises with him. He said the shop was under--used and I could have one side for my wallpaper books and the other would be used for the stationery stuff, pictures and posters. He had his print office out the back and he constantly had to go between that and the front of the shop for customers. If I was out front, I could look after the stationery side as well and that could be offset against any rent. It seemed a perfect solution for both of us, and we started to expand on the way we could work together, and I got carried away with enthusiasm and spoke for some time then I suddenly remembered Jan still waiting in the car, she would not be happy. I made my excuses and hurried back. Jan was furious – she complained she had been stuck in the car with all the shopping and dying to return home to use the toilet. She hadn't dared to leave the car with all the shopping there and she had expected me to get back at any minute. She had a clear view of our house across the valley, adding to her feeling of frustrated and entrapment. She cared nothing for my excuses, or my news, she just wanted to get home. We drove back in silence.

***

Later that evening I explained my conversation with Doug to her, but I could see how upset and disappointment she was. "You have done it again!" she said, and went on to explain she believed this was going to be a new start for both of us to find work together, and I had ruined everything. I protested that nothing changed that, believing this would be the perfect opportunity to start afresh together and the shop premises would serve very well as a business for the both of us. But my conversation with Doug clearly bothered her, and she said she did not want to work with "this Doug person", she thought it would be just the two of us together. Now she said she didn't care what I did, the moment had gone and she had changed her mind and didn't want to work with me after all. I said that was silly and we could still do things the way we had planned, but she said no, I would always be going off on tangents and she realized that is just the way I was. I felt bad that I had spoilt thing for her and I just hoped she would come round once I got the shop up and running. But she never did, not in the way I had originally conceived, but it seemed she would end up **getting her own back,** in a way that I was totally unprepared for.

***

For the moment though I felt I needed to get my business started and also to get the extension built, as Jan's mum and dad started to show signs of frustration at not living in their own space, especially Jan's mum. Jan's dad loved Cornwall and the surroundings, but her mum constantly complained to him and got him riled up too. He had also upset her by declaring after the drive down to Cornwall, that he was going to retire from driving. Since Jan's mum didn't drive, this was very annoying to her, especially when he announced he intended to give the car to Colin (Jan's brother). As it happened Colin refused the offer, his business really succeeded and he could afford to buy new cars for both he and his wife, Sally.

***

Still hopeful Jan would come round; I went to settle things with Doug. We would call the shop 'Doodles and Design' and he would continue to print in the office at the back, while I looked after the shop. On one side I would display all my wall covering books and fabrics with samples, and on the other side we would stock Doug's items of stationary along with the usual postcards and large posters depicting Cornish themes with some special jokey ones designed by a friend of Doug's, Nick Burridge, and some paintings on the wall from local artists. The printing would be totally Doug's province and the wall coverings, fabrics and design service totally mine. All the other stuff we would share 50/50. In addition I had brought down with me an exclusive agency for Cornwall from 3M's for Scotchguard carpet protection, which really interested Doug, so I said he could share the agency with me once we were established, and it would mean one of us going up to a seminar at 3M's in a few months' time when the product was going to be launched. I also would arrange for Malcolm to build the counters in the shop needed for my wall covering library. Having agreed all between us, I promised start in the shop as soon as I sorted out the extension on the house.

CHAPTER 3

HILARY AND MALCOM

The building regulations came through in the middle of March and I contacted Malcolm to start on the footings. I would help him on the dig and soon we laboured away digging down the trenches. Malcolm and I got on well; we liked the same music and shared the same sense of humour. At the end of one day, when I went home, hot and tired, Jan said, "I see you've got another friend," and I'm sure I detected a touch of bitterness in her voice, so I suggested she go and chat with Malcolm, as I am sure she would like him. Initially a bit shy as always, gradually she came to speak with him, first to take tea and then Malcolm would talk to her when he took the tea things back, and I could see he turned on the charm. As he became more familiar, I noticed him flirting with her, much to Jan's appreciation. I only felt glad; as I could see it boosted her spirits and brought her out of her shell. Once we completed the footings Malcolm made a start on my counters in the shop. As I said before, Malcolm was very good looking and when he was in the shop, Doug's girlfriend, Maggie, dropped in and started chatting with him, but I noticed he didn't pay her the same attention as he did to Jan. It surprised me as I think it also did Maggie. She was the local beauty in Aggie (St.Agnes), and with her long black hair and her tanned and toned figure, she was used to having many admirers. While Malcolm was working on the counters one day, Ruth Williams, a very good local artist, came into the shop. She was quite a flamboyant middle aged woman, and when she saw Malcolm stripped off to the waist working on his carpentry, she stood gazing at him. Then she told him she was painting a picture of Christ's crucifixion and Malcolm looked perfect for the part of Jesus, as he looked so much like the depictions of him seen in the churches. The fact that he was a carpenter clinched it, and she asked him if he

would pose for her, she would pay him the going rate. Malcolm agreed but we never did see the end picture.
***

Once Malcolm completed the counters he could return to recruiting his team to start building the extension, and I to work in the shop. I fixed up my wall covering books and updated on a few others and got fresh samples. I just finished sorting out the display when Doug asked me if I wanted to go for a ride. It had been one of the really hot weeks we occasionally endured in the beginning of May and the temperature outside was as sultry as any summers day. We shut up shop and Doug drove me down to Chapel Porth to see if the surf was up. Doug had been one of the original surfers with the long board when they first arrived in Cornwall and like all surfers, nothing mattered more than a good swell. When the summer came I would get used to his frequent disappearances and the string of irate customers fed up with waiting for their printing to be completed. His girlfriend Maggie was also an expert surfer. She had been married previously to a local businessman and they had a couple of children. They all lived down near the beach in a bungalow called 'Goofy- Foot' named after Maggie's left footed surfing stance. I found out later, that she and Doug had a brief affair, and then she emigrated with her husband to Canada; but the marriage didn't last, and then she returned to pursue Doug again. At first, Doug played hard to get, maybe because she hurt him before by leaving him to go with her husband to Canada, but to me, he just claimed she was too old now and why did he want someone older for a girlfriend. Only three years older than him and the same age as me, she was still a very fanciable woman. It was all talk on his part however, as they eventually got back together.
***

When we arrived at Chapel Porth, Doug took me down on to the beach and soon we were surrounded by a bevy of bikini clad girls. Doug introduced them as the vicar's four daughters and their friends, and the next thing

I knew we were all playing volleyball together on the beach. I thought this must beat working anywhere.

***

Back at the house Jan's mum was being difficult and grumbling about everything. Jan and I mistakenly thought it would be like the 'Walton's', a popular television program about a Midwest family living in the Blue Ridge mountains of America, with three generations of a family all living happily under the one roof and sharing everything with the parents, children and lovable grandparents. It wasn't at all like that and to Jan's mum everything was wrong. She said she was used to living in her own space and she had given up her lovely bungalow to live on a building site. I tried to explain this was all temporary and soon she would enjoy a lovely place of her own again all brand spanking new, but nothing pleased her much to Jan's misery. Malcolm mentioned to me he felt sorry for Jan as she had to put up with so much from her mother, and he suggested we go out with him and his girlfriend one evening for a drink, to break the monotony for Jan. It sounded like a good idea, Mark was eleven and Troy was nine, and I asked them if they would look after Adam and Simon with Nanny and Granddad one evening while we went out. Gladys, Jan's mum, reluctantly agreed to keep an eye on the children to make sure everything was alright.

***

So with that settled, the next day I suggested I pick up Malcolm and his girlfriend from their house on the following Saturday, and we go for a drive and find a nice little country pub. My car was garaged for an MOT, and Jan's dad offered his car as he wasn't driving it anymore, he thought of selling it. I found that Malcolm lived in a little old terraced cottage at the back of Truro, apparently his girlfriend's house. The cottage was quaint and dark inside and the dining room and lounge were open plan, separated by an arch. The furniture was minimal, with just a dining room suite, and bean-bags with cushions on the floor of the lounge. Malcolm introduced us to Hilary, his girlfriend, and I was surprised to find that she was a very elegant, attractive blonde with the most strikingly beautiful blue eyes. Her poise and bearing gave away her training as a dancer, first in ballet and then in a chorus line and her whole face lit up when she smiled. Her sophisticated look juxtaposed against Malcolm's rugged appearance and they looked ill matched, but I reckoned she fell for his looks and earthy charm. Apparently, she had left her husband, a successful local businessman, for Malcolm, running off with him, after he spent time at their house, building an extension. Should I have thought more about that?

***

We drove to the Smugglers Inn near Cubert and we all enjoyed each other. Hillary and I got on especially well together as we seemed to share a lot of similar interests. She liked books, art and poetry, and had a particularly love of history, with special interest in the local history of Cornwall. Jan joined in our conversation when she wasn't being chatted up by Malcolm, who seemed fixated with her as the evening wore on. Hillary didn't seem to mind, and instead focused all her attention on me, and perhaps complimenting me a little too much. I began to feel slightly uneasy, when Jan said, "My goodness look at the time, it is a quarter to twelve already." Malcolm said the pubs weren't fussy about the time so not to worry, but I still had to run them back to Truro. When we got to the car and started it up the petrol gauge showed nearly empty as I had meant to refuel on the way to the pub, but I completely forgot. It was touch and go whether I had enough to go all the way to Truro and back to St. Agnes. In those days it was unusual for garages to be open all night, especially in Cornwall, but Malcolm assured us he knew of a garage in Indian Queens open all the time. I hoped he was right as Indian Queens lie in the opposite direction and a trip there would only use up much of the little petrol left if we found no open garage. When we reached the garage at Indian Queens it was shut, and now I really worried. We definitely didn't have enough petrol to get back and all the

garages were shut. Malcolm said not to worry and invited us to stay over if we could just reach their place in Truro. However, Jan said her mum would never help her out again if we did that, while I confessed my doubt the car carried enough fuel to get to Truro anyway. We drove along the A30 and just entering Marazanvose when I saw a light in a shed set well back from the road. I turned up the track and it led to an old garage workshop. I got out of the car and went in, startling the man inside, but I apologised straight away and told him of my predicament. He said he was sorry but he didn't sell petrol and owned no pumps. I asked for any spare cans with just a little in, and while he said no, he then thought for a minute. "I've just remembered I had to drain a car this morning and there might be a little in an old bowl somewhere." He hunted round the workshop and returned with the old bowl with about half a gallon of petrol swilling around in it, and found a funnel. "There you are," he said, "You can have that". What a relief, he had saved us and I was willing to pay him handsomely for it. I asked him how much I should pay him, but he asked for nothing, as he was just glad to make use of it he said. I thanked him profusely, and then got Malcolm to help pour it in while I held the funnel, it would do, but we couldn't afford to lose a drop, and then we were on our way. After dropping off Malcolm and Hillary, we sped home, not looking forward to what Jan's mum would have to say to us. When I opened the front door I was astonished to see Adam and Simon on the stairs. They rushed down asking us where we were and thinking mummy and daddy had left them. Everybody in the house was fast asleep, and then Jan found her mum's door was locked. So much for her babysitting: Jan couldn't believe it and said it was most unfair as she never normally went out and now she didn't feel she could again.
***
As regards the car incident I had another in some ways similar event several months later in the Opel. I drove up with Jan and the children to stay with my mum and dad in St. Albans. It was Mark and Troy's half-term holiday in

November and quite bleak and cold. At the end of the week Jan caught a cold and the children picked up a tummy-bug, but come the Sunday we needed to get back as next day mean school for the children and a follow up business meeting in London for me. Anyway we couldn't get away until the afternoon with everyone feeling under the weather and we just crossed over the Bristol flyover from the M4 to the M5 when my front tyre blew making controlling the car quite difficult. Once onto the hard shoulder, I managed to change the wheel and we set off again only to run into a traffic jam caused by an accident. The children felt ill and everyone was fed up. In those days, without the improvements to the A30 through Devon, the quickest route back ran over the Tamar Bridge, and with all the delays we reached Cornwall past 11.30 pm. I drove just on the Liskeard by-pass when another tyre blew, nearing midnight on a wet and cold November Sunday night; and all those years ago at the time Cornwall was closed. It was before the days of mobile phones and there was no telephone box in sight. My ripped spare tyre left no way of getting home. To make matters worse, four sick children and a sick wife felt wretched and heavy with cold. I was miles from the nearest houses and the roads were deserted. I didn't know what to do. I had pulled the car over on to a verge just past a lane where Castle Air was later to build their works but was still a few years away. I decided to get out and walk down the lane to see if I could find a house although I didn't know who I was going to phone even if I did. The first thing I saw when I turned into the lane was the old Castle Motors scrap yard, but at that time of night it was closed. Then right at the back I saw a dim light and when I tried the gate it opened. I walked up to the shed where I saw the light and found a man inside doing some paperwork. I explained to him my predicament and asked if he carried a spare wheel I could buy. He asked what make of car I and said an Opel Rekord wasn't a common make of car, doubting he had a wheel to fit. Then he checked his papers and said I was in luck they might just have one as long as it hadn't been crushed yet. With a torch we clambered over the pile of wrecked cars and there precariously balance near the top was an Opel Rekord, but to my dismay all the wheels had gone. He said, "Sorry mate I can't help you, obviously the wheels have been sold separately and I know they are not in the stores." Dejectedly we climbed back down again and then he said "It's probably a long shot, but I suppose we could just check the boot," and sure enough there was the spare wheel with fully blown up tyre. I couldn't believe my luck and asked him if I could buy it, half expecting a high price as I was desperate and would pay anything in reason. "You can have it for 50p," he said, "and I hope it gets you home. I thanked him profusely and rushed back to the car with the wheel. Already resigned herself to us all spending an extremely uncomfortable night in the car, Jan breathed a sigh of relief when I returned with a wheel. We put it on and made it home without further incident.

***

We all loved our life in Cornwall; oh well, with the exception of Jan's mum. Mark and Troy loved their school and they very quickly made friends there, many of whom remain good friends with them and the whole family all these years later. As for the school, it was not so academically advanced as their school in Harpenden and they could coast through the lessons being far ahead of their classmates. The whole atmosphere of the school was relaxed and the teachers were kind and good, especially the Headmaster, Mr. Mitchell who served for the first few years. Jan and I remember passing the school playground and there he was with a chain of little children hanging on to each arm as he turned them round and round, and Troy remembers being sent to the Headmaster for some minor misdemeanor once, Mr. Mitchell felt sorry for him as he looked so worried, and after Troy promised never to repeat again what got him into trouble, Mr. Mitchell discreetly sent him to the shop to buy some sweets. He was a lovely kindly man, but unfortunately he suffered a minor stroke and had to leave after a couple of years.

***

Adam and Simon were happy at playschool, although the other women there weren't friendly to Jan. They misinterpreted Jan's shyness for a snobbish reserve and saw her as an outsider. We learnt later that we had purchased the house that the mother of the woman running the local playschool had been after before we came along, and for some reason felt we had undercut her. Only Corelie, a woman who lived close by, went out of her way to be friendly to Jan. But for all that, Jan loved Cornwall and the beauty of it all, and our walks with all the family at weekends were just lovely. Her dad was happy as long as he could work in the allotment he had made from a patch in the back garden and keep out of the way of Jan's mum. That first hot summer, working in the shop in the village, was also a tonic for me, seeing all the holiday makers and chatting to Doug and popping home at lunchtime to see Jan, and Malcolm with his fellow workers. They were also a diversion for Jan and the children. They were all very friendly and enjoyed watching and bantering with Adam and Simon.

***

One day I was up in the shop and I heard this voice say "I don't believe it, it's Ronnie. What on earth are you doing here?" It was Andy Lazelle, Don Ellis's secretary from the Czech agency. We had always got on so well together and she had come to see my Peacock Arts exhibitions in the De Vere hotel and we had spent a lot of time in each other's company at work. If the truth be known if Jan hadn't existed Andy would have definitely been my Number One. As it was she was second only to Jan and here she was with her husband and looking about seven months pregnant. She asked if I could join them across the road at the St. Agnes Hotel for a drink as she was thrilled to bump in to me, but they were going home the next day. I checked with Doug and joined them across at the pub. Andy wanted to know all I had been up to and how I had ended up down there, in Cornwall of all places. I pointed out my house, which could be seen across the valley and I gave her a sketchy biography, to which she said that nothing surprised her, and they had all said at the agency I would either end up a millionaire or in prison. Anyway, she was pleased it wasn't the latter but sorry it wasn't the former. I then asked her all about herself and she told me after I left she left she worked for a firm locally in Grays Thurrock where she lived and that she had recently married, I could see the result. The rapport between us was still there and we were laughing and joking about old times when I noticed the black look on her husband's face. Poor man, we had been so wrapped up in our conversation that we had rudely left him out. I apologised to him, but Andy said, "Oh ignore him, old misery guts," and he, understandably continued sitting there with his sulky look. Then he got up and said to her they had to go as there were other places to visit. Andy looked at me, smiled and shrugged she said, "Oh well I better go, but it was so lovely seeing you and we must keep in touch now I've found you." I reciprocated and said it would be great. A couple of weeks later I received a lovely letter from her saying how thrilled she was to see me and we must keep in touch. However, a few days later when I wanted to write back to her I couldn't find her letter anywhere or trace her address, so I never was able to reply.

***

The next day Malcolm suggested at the weekend, Jan and I with the children meet up with him and Hillary and go for a walk across the fields to the Passage Inn on the Helford Passage. It was a lovely sunny day and Malcolm took a ball and had a kick around with the boys which amused them, and then with a play fight in the long grass. When we reached the pub we all sat outside in the sunshine watching the boats on the river. Then Hillary asked me how the business had been on my wall coverings, fabrics and interior design service through the summer. I had to admit that it had been pretty poor. I had sold some stuff and had a few visitors from the adverts but it wasn't really going anywhere. She said it was a shame as she loved the idea and would like to participate, but she said St. Agnes was too remote and I needed a shop in Truro, the only real shopping centre in Cornwall. She knew someone who could find me some premises she went on. He was a bit creepy and she didn't like him, but she had also worked with his wife who was lovely. Anyway this chap knew where to find any shop premises selling in Truro, and she said she would love to work with me and run the Truro shop if I wanted. Malcolm could fit it out and she wouldn't take a wage, but share in the profits if it would help. Everyone seemed to think it was a good idea, and I said suggested a partnership among Malcolm, Hillary, Jan and me and call it 'Ideas in Design'. Hillary and I would run the shops and consult on designs with Jan when possible, Malcolm could execute any practical work needed including painting and decorating if required, and Jan and I would keep the books. Jan cautioned us to not rush into things and to think it through, but Malcolm and Hillary reacted very enthusiastically. When we got home Jan said that she thought that I was giving everything away as usual. She liked Malcolm and Hillary and she could see where I was coming from, trying to expand again without money but it would be my ideas that everyone was cashing in on. I reminded her that I hadn't been discharged from bankruptcy and I needed a front. Also by sharing the load I could spend more time with her, but we had to locate premises before anything could begin.

***

I was sitting talking to Doug outside the St. Agnes Hotel (the 'Aggie') one sunny lunchtime, it was the tail end of summer, when his girlfriend Maggie, came out of the pub and poured a full pint glass of beer over his head and said, "I hope you and your friend" (indicating me) "will be very happy together," and then she stormed off. It appeared he paid more attention to me than to her. Anyway, Doug just seemed to ignore it and carried on talking to me as if nothing happened. I must have looked pretty shocked but he offered no explanation.

***

I just secured the premises in Truro, and John Wellings lived up to Hillary's description a strange fellow. The premises rented out at a low price, but were stuck up a side road, Kenwyn Street off Victoria Square; but it just had a doorway with no windows, or as I described it with concrete windows. Hillary reckoned we could display and advertise on the walls and it should bring the people into the shop. I spent what little money I earned through the summer on books, samples and advertising, but the shop was not yet up and running, and business almost stopped in the Aggie shop. Doug said someone asked him to move a piano and if I might help. He could borrow a van from someone who assembled barrel furniture and she would pay us to take the piano away. I noted how funny that was, a piano seemed a nuisance to someone who wanted to dispose of it, but a treasure to someone who wanted one. Then I hit on an idea. Why don't we run two advertisements, one offering pianos for sale and one, with a different number offering to dispose of unwanted pianos. We could use this job of Doug's, as a test case. Doug drafted an advert to publish in the local West Briton newspaper offering a piano for sale and five people enquired. With a lot of effort we managed to collect the one Doug offered for a charge of £25 and described its details to the enquirers, and they all replied with interest and we accepted offers, the highest of which was £75. So we made £100 on our first deal less petrol and a couple of beers for the van owner. In all we repeated the procedure on 14 pianos and the worst by far was collecting one from a little cottage in St. Ives. At one time we thought we were going to have to take the window out, but eventually with a lot of back and forth and twisting and turning, we finally removed it and loaded it on to the lorry. That was the main trouble: the pianos were very heavy and each collection and delivery left us completely shattered. Still in all we made a little over £1,000 in clear profit in a very short space of time and then Doug's friend's van failed the MOT and he got rid of it. We didn't feel inclined to invest in a new van and anyway, we decided it was all a bit too much like hard work.

***

Then the rep. from 3M's came down to see us about the agency I had for Scotchguard and invited us up to a demonstration that was being given as a one day course in Maidstone, Kent. I was too busy with the new Truro shop but Doug said he would go and he came back full of enthusiasm. He wanted us to start a carpet cleaning company using the Scotchguard process as our market leader and he said that 3M's were about to launch a massive advertising campaign. With most of our piano money we invested in the necessary equipment that Doug had seen on his course and initially he said he would use his Volvo estate to carry it around. We called the company 'Magic Carpets' and Doug said he would conduct the cleaning if I would administrate and bookkeep. Doug's method of accounts with his print business had been to put all the demands for money in a tray, then when he got paid for a job he would shuffle the tray, pick out an envelope and pay it. Consequently he had a combination of bills and writs in his tray and he always kept a reserve for bailiffs to pay them off when they called. The adverts coupled with the leads from 3M's kept the enquiries coming in and soon Doug was very busy going here, there and everywhere cleaning and Scotchguarding carpets. I took the enquiries, scheduled the appointments and drafted the invoices when required and also ensured that the supplies of cleaning fluid and Scotchguard were always there. However, Doug performed all the donkey work and rushing around, and I grew increasingly busier with 'Ideas in Design'. Then one day after work Doug asked to change the partnership, as most of the work fell on him and therefore so should more of the profit. I agreed, as things seemed escalated on the design front as will be explained later I said I would surrender my shares for nothing and he could have all the company himself and perhaps he could get Maggie to do the bits and pieces I had been doing. To his credit Doug worked very hard on the business and built it up into a thriving little company, which he was eventually able to sell when he and Maggie eventually immigrated to Australia.

***

At the beginning of June 1977 St. Agnes held its first Victorian Fair to commemorate the Queen's Jubilee, 25 years since she first came to the throne. It was held on the Whitsun Bank Holiday and was quite a big affair. There were stalls all through the village with the stall holders in Victorian costume and also quite a few of the locals in costume too, including Doug and Maggie. There was a steam organ and a steam engine and a wet sponge to throw at the local headmaster who was in the stocks, there were Morris Dancers, St. Agnes Silver Band, a children's Merry-Go-Round, and a try-your-strength hammer and gong, a pasty competition and many other attractions including a Caribbean Band in Peterville later. Jan and I went up with the children and Jan's mum and dad accompanied us. We met Malcolm and Hilary with some of their friends and also Doug and Maggie. Everybody seemed to be enjoying themselves and the sun was shining. Mark and Troy met up with some of their school friends and all the rest of us congregated round the Aggie. Everything was so relaxed and friendly and we felt really at home in St. Agnes even though it had been a mere matter of months. By the summer Jan's parents flat was finally finished. The workmen Malcolm had employed had done a very good job and especially the block work and plastering carried out by Tony Gardner who was an extremely clean and competent craftsman, but plumbers, electricians carpenters and labourers had all worked well and Malcolm had taken a special pride in ensuring we wouldn't be disappointed. Even Jan's mum couldn't really find much to criticise in the end product.

***

One Sunday in late September I decided to take Jan and the children out for a ride to St. Mawes about 20 miles away. Sundays in Cornwall in those days out, of the holiday season, were very quiet and there was hardly any traffic on the road. We had been used to the busy roads of Hertfordshire for our Sunday drives and walks and Jan said "What does everybody in Cornwall do on a Sunday?" We couldn't believe how empty everywhere was. Anyway we all went for a nice walk round St. Mawes and along the estuary and on our way back we bought the boys ice-creams and then started on our way home. I was just approaching Ruan High Lanes just out of St. Mawes when I tried to slow the car into a bend and found that I had no brakes, my foot just sunk to the floor with no response. It was Sunday evening and in those days in Cornwall everywhere was shut so I decided I would have to drive back using my hand-brake to stop or slow the car. I just approached the main road from St. Austell to Truro and pulled up the hand-brake to stop when the cable snapped. I had four hungry kids in the car all wanting their dinner and it would soon be Adam and Simon's bedtime. It was in the days before mobile phones and credit cards. I had no change for the phone and no money to arrange any alternative way home for us all. As there was hardly any traffic on the road I decided to risk it, taking the back lanes and using my gears to slow the car. If I really came across an emergency I would have to scrape the car on the verge to bring it to a stop. It was my lucky day, I never came across any other cars to cause me trouble and I was able to cross the junctions with the only traffic to be seen in the distance. However when I got to Goonbell and Goonown in St. Agnes I was suddenly in a built up area with parked cars all along the side and a downhill road. I took it very gingerly and had almost made it home when round the corner at Rosemundy I met a car coming the other way expecting me to stop but I couldn't. It was then I had to scrape the car on the wall to bring it to a stop damaging the wing. After that I did the last part of the journey in first gear at a crawl and then we were safely home. Jan and the boys remembered that nightmare ride for a long time. The poor old Opel was now on its last legs and I felt wouldn't be lasting me much longer but I would have to get the brakes repaired as I couldn't afford to buy another car.

***

In the meantime I was running down the St. Agnes shop for the little shop in Truro which was ticking over well, but I would miss the village in the summer, watching all the tourists and popping back at lunchtime, rushing out every time we had a shower of rain to bring in the poster and card racks outside the shop. We had one or two good contracts on the design business such as the 'Idle Rocks' hotel in St. Mawes and Trewithen, after several rooms had caught fire, and Hillary was doing a very good job of running it, but we were not getting enough custom to earn a good living from it and was only just about covering the costs and the wage I had insisted that Hillary took. Then in August, Jan, I, and the four boys all went shopping in Plymouth mainly to buy Mark his birthday present and a belated one for Troy. I was amazed at the crowds there compared with Truro and then the boys saw a few people who they knew from school and they said that really Plymouth was the main shopping centre for people from Cornwall. I remarked to Jan that if we really wanted to make 'Ideas in Design' work, then we needed a shop in Plymouth, but when I investigated rent prices and deposits there was no way I could afford it. I had to get into Plymouth somehow and wracked my brains to try to think of a way.

CHAPTER 4

THINKING BIG/DEBENHAMS

I was sleeping, eating, and thinking of whatever I must do to bring in more revenue, I had an idea. Debenhams was by far the biggest store in Plymouth and they had loads of floor space. I would write to their head office to suggest that I rent a counter in their wallpaper section with my own display of expensive wall coverings and fabrics. I would supply everything that was needed and also staff to run the counter. It would cost them nothing and I would give them a 25% of the profits made on all sales with a minimum guaranteed payment at the end of a six month trial period. If it worked I would expect a longer term contract.

***

I sent the letter off to the Head Office marked for the attention of the Sales Director, not really expecting a reply. Then to my amazement after a couple of weeks I had a letter inviting me to a meeting with their Board of Directors in November, when I could expound on my ideas. Hence, we took a trip to my parent home in St.Albans to drop off the children and went on to attend the Debenhams meeting. I was confronted by five members of the Board, the Managing Director, and the Sales Director, the Marketing Director, the Chief Accountant and the Director in charge of Administration plus a secretary to take notes. They made up an arc in front of me behind the Directors huge desk and I sat on a chair in front of them all and was asked to go through my proposal. As I talked I could see that they were smiling to each other but I didn't know if it was because they thought I was being ridiculous or they were amused at my impertinence. Then when I finished, they asked me to leave and wait outside whilst they discussed the matter between themselves. After about quarter of an hour I was summoned back in by the secretary and I had no idea what to expect. Once I was seated the Managing Director cupped his hands and rested his chin in them with his elbows on the desk and just stared at me for several minutes. Then he sat upright and said that the idea intrigued them and they would like to give it a trial but on the understanding that if it worked they would like me to gradually phase it in over all 78 of their stores, but my idea needed some refining. Firstly, I would be responsible for employing whatever staff I thought fit and the employment contract would be between my company and my employee. I said that I expected that. Secondly they said that I would be responsible for constructing my own counters and organising all my own display, but it would have to submit to store manager approval. I said such protocol would not present a problem. Finally they said that all the takings at the till would be collected by them, a n d whoever I employed would collect payment through their staff structure but deducted from my income as would any other incidental expenses I had incurred. They would give me the necessary paperwork to be filled in to show the purchase price of all goods sold. From this calculation having taken all the running and purchase costs into account they would deduct 40% of the residue and reimburse me with the balance. I baulked at the 40% and said that I thought that it was excessive as I still had to deal with my establishment costs, buying the books, building the counters etc. The Sales Director then said they would not consider the idea for anything less than 40% and that I had proved that I had a very persuasive argument and if I was so sure of the sort of sales I predicted I could borrow the money from the bank and it would quickly be recouped. I said that I still thought that they drove a hard bargain, but perhaps when I had proved myself and they had seen the success of my venture we could renegotiate. The Managing Director just said "Perhaps" and then "So we have a deal", I agreed and he said his legal team would prepare the necessary paperwork and that they would program it in to start immediately after the January sales, around the middle of January which would give me two weeks to get my team in, immediately after the Christmas and New Year, to get everything up and running for the launch. Then we all shook hands and I left. When I got back and told Jan the good news she said "Oh dear what have you got yourself into now." When I got home there was a letter waiting for me from the Official Receiver saying that in the light of news that they had been given, an application by me to be discharged from bankruptcy would be favourably received. So I was to get an early discharge after just three years instead of the usual five that was mandatory in those days, unless you repaid a major part of your indebtedness. So this was good new indeed as I needed to apply for a bank loan.

CHAPTER 5

INSPECTOR LEE CAME TO ARREST ME.

On the following Monday when I went into Truro to tell Hillary all about my Debenhams meeting, she informed me that an Inspector Lee had called at the shop to see me and would be returning on the following Thursday. Apparently he had called at the house but Jan's mum hadn't known who he was and assumed that he was to do with the business, referring him to Doug, who referred him to Hillary. On the Thursday I made sure that I was in the shop to await the arrival of Inspector Lee, feeling a little apprehensive. What could go wrong now? He arrived at midday, he was a slightly portly man in his fifties and he was dressed in plain clothes. He asked me if he could take me to lunch and suggested the Chinese restaurant across the road. I still hadn't a clue what it was all about and although I answered his friendly manner in as polite a way as I could, I was still very suspicious. Then as we finished our lunch he started recounting a story to me that I found almost impossible to believe. He started off by saying that he believed I had an interest in a firm called Inland Alkaloids, and I responded that my only interest had been to find them, as they had swindled me out of £56,000 worth of Ergotamine Tartrate. Then he asked me how well I knew Billy Hitchcock, and I told him that I had only met him briefly when I went to San Francisco to get him to invest £10,000 in my Animal Feed Business. He then said are you sure it wasn't an additional £42,000($100,000) on the promise that you would supply him with LSD? I said that was ridiculous, the only way I could supply anyone with Lysergic Acid was with an end user certificate and I had not even discussed supplying it to them. All I had received into my account was the £10,000 and I could show the legal agreement that had been entered into for that. If it hadn't been for the fraud perpetrated on my company, it would have been very successful and Billy

Hitchcock would have got his loan back with the agreed interest. As it was, I had lost a very good business and ended up bankrupt and had moved to Cornwall for a fresh start. He then asked me about Mike Druce and asked if during our visit he had been left alone with Billy Hitchcock and his cohorts. I said that only on the one day that I was ill with an upset stomach; I had spent the day in my bedroom. He then leaned back in his chair and said, "I'm going to tell you a little story…

***

Firstly, I don't know whether it was you or Druce, or both of you together. I think from the stories I have heard you were probably too naïve to work by yourself, so let's say it was either Druce acting by himself, or with your knowledge. The people you met in San Francisco call themselves 'The Brotherhood of Eternal Love' and their one purpose is to make hallucinatory drugs available on the market to anyone who wants them. Cutting out the idealistic crap, they are in it for the money. Anyway, on the understanding that you were to supply them with LSD or Lysergic Acid from Czechoslovakia, they transferred to Mike Druce, £42,000 ($100,000). But after two years they still hadn't received a single delivery, so they started putting the pressure on. Luckily for Druce, the march of chemical science had moved on in those two years and LSD could then be synthesised from Ergotamine Tartrate which Druce duly supplied to them. From what you tell me, I assume by what followed after, you had no knowledge of. Anyway, everything was going smoothly until you started sending out letters to many of the members of the Brotherhood, demanding money or you would go to the police. They tried threatening you and your family, but you seemed adamant in going through with it. They then sent one of their men, a Professor Ronald Stark, with the brief to see if you should be eliminated. Luckily for you Mr. Craze, he reported back to them that you weren't worth the trouble and that you had probably done all you were going to do. However, because

the letters had been widely circulated to people, possibly outside the Brotherhood, they decided to close their manufacturing plant in the South of France, take a two year sabbatical and then reopen in North Wales where some reliable members of the Brotherhood lived and they would start a new production line. Some members weren't happy however, and thought that some action should be taken against you, but I assume whatever they thought or planned, could not have come too anything. Mr. Craze, by your actions you skated on very thin ice and are lucky to still be here. We discovered all this when we raided their offices in Switzerland and froze their bank account. It was all part of 'Operation Julie' and we have now raided the Welsh factory and have them all in custody. Our Associates in the States are mopping up the various individuals over there. Most of what I have said was contained in the Minutes of the Brotherhood which we discovered in their safe deposit box in Switzerland and the International Drug Agency pressurized the Swiss to co-operate. I came down here to see if I should arrest you Mr. Craze, but I think that you were a small pawn whom was probably duped and I don't believe the Ergotamine was supplied with your consent. So as far as I can see you have just been very foolish but it seems you supplied nothing, so I will leave it there." We then got up to go and once out of the restaurant, he shook my hand and thanked me for my co-operation. Then as he was leaving, he called back "By the way, I loved the bit about you offering your 'Woodbines' in exchange for a joint", (so my embarrassing story was out), I called back to him, "n o t Woodbines, it was Benson and Hedges', but he had gone.
***

This little interview answered a lot of questions for me. In my head, it drew the final line under my old London life, and I could now concentrate on my new life in Cornwall. I had an exciting new project to prepare and very little time to get everything sorted out.

CHAPTER 6

NOW TO GET ON WITH BUSINESS

I had been in Cornwall just a matter of months and already I had gone from a shop in St. Agnes to one in Truro and now in Plymouth. Not to mention an interview with a Policeman who was wondering whether to arrest me; a lot of things had happened.

***

First I had to arrange a bank loan to buy everything necessary for the new project in Debenhams. With Malcolm building the counters and duplicates of the Truro books with a few samples, to hire a staff, I could probably get away with a little over £3,000 and an additional £2,000 to ensure that we had wages in hand in case business was slow. That weekend Jan and I met with Malcolm and Hilary at our house to discuss the way forward. We agreed we would open an account for 'Ideas in Design' with Lloyds Bank in Perranporth where Jan had her account. The four of us would meet with the bank manager armed with the contract from Debenhams to try to open an account with a £5,000 overdraft, although they were all adamant that I did the talking.

***

I showed Malcolm my design for the counter I wanted in Debenhams to be made out of white laminated chipboard and I suggested he and I go up to Plymouth in a couple of weeks before Christmas to talk to the manager and see where he wanted the counter to be and to take measurements and get the materials ordered. Hilary said that she would see to ordering all the books but she and Jan ought to go as well to assess the situation, we could make it on a Monday as the Truro shop would be closed. She also suggested that I meet with a broker called Keith Turner who arranged finance for her ex. husband as if matters took off we would need back up finance.

***

Finally, we agreed immediately after Christmas we should start advertising for staff to run the Debenhams outlet. We managed to get an appointment to see the bank manager on the Wednesday, but despite my best efforts he would only allow us a £3,000 loan to get started which was less than we needed. I decided then to contact Keith Turner to see if there was any possibility of getting alternative finance to top it up. Christmas 1977 was fast approaching and with Debenhams wanting us to be up and running by the end of January time was slipping away.

***

I got round to seeing Keith Turner a week before Christmas in his Office, overlooking High Cross in Truro. He was one of those people I had an instant rapport with and he was to become a good friend. He was a tall, well-built man with thinning black curly hair, a ruddy complexion and a trim beard. He was the hale and hearty type, loud and extrovert, always with a joke and a ready laugh. I explained to him what I was about and he thought it was a fantastic idea. Then he asked me about my background and feeling at ease I started to tell him, but as I saw his mouth drop open I thought I better cut back on the story and just give him edited highlights. However this was enough. Obviously my cavalier attitude to business, far from putting him off, seemed to make him more and more enthusiastic to work with me and even with only 50% of my story he seemed to think it was incredible and he told me to leave things with him and he would definitely be able to sort something out for me by the New Year.

He then asked if I would stay on for a while as some of his business associates were coming round for an office Christmas drink and I was welcome to join them. I was just about to make my apologies and leave, when people started turning up and I was introduced in typical overstated Keith fashion with "You won't believe this guy – he's incredible. Just wait till he tells you his story". I demurred and said that it's not really that incredible but Keith persisted that I regale those present with my story. I was embarrassed, here were people I didn't know and in my eyes my story seemed to show me as a bit of a loser and wally, an impression I didn't wish to give. I remember some of the others as Keith's business partner, Roy Hunt and his wife or girlfriend, the solicitor Noel Horner, another solicitor Brian Bennett, a guy called John Osborne, Keith's secretary (who was very nice and considerate to me, trying to put me at ease) and another couple of blokes whose names I can't remember. Anyway the wine and the drink started flowing and having given them a brief run down as I had given Keith; I started to wish I was somewhere else. Then someone started passing round a large joint. I had never even smoked a joint up until then and when it was offered I declined but they all insisted and under pressure I decided to join in. However, after a few puffs I started feeling quite sick. Everybody else seemed to be drifting off and I was just feeling ill. I made my excuses and said that I must get going. Nobody seemed that aware, so I quietly drifted out and left them.

CHAPTER 7

WE HAVE GONE TOO FAR

Drawn more together by our partnership, Jan and I saw a lot of Malcolm and Hilary. They would pop round at weekends and we would go for walks together with the children. On rare occasions we would meet in Truro for a drink in the evening but Jan was always anxious to hurry home. She still didn't altogether trust her mum with the babysitting. Now with Debenhams looming we were to become more and more involved with each other. Malcolm was always flirting and joking with Jan and I could see that she loved the attention and by way of compensation, Hilary seemed to have a fixation with me. I could do nothing wrong in her eyes and the way she would look at me with those beautiful blue eyes made me feel faintly uneasy. With Malcolm and Jan it seemed more light-hearted fun I thought, but there was an intensity in the way Hilary reacted to me and I in turn found her to be interesting and knowledgeable about the things that fascinated me, as well as being extremely attractive. It was my feeling that the situation that was beginning to disturb me, and Jan was too busy with Malcolm to notice, then came the weekend before Christmas.

***

Malcolm and Hilary suggested we ask Jan's mum to baby-sit and that we go for a drink in Truro and back to their house for a meal. The drink consisted of a Christmas sing-song in the Navy Arms by candlelight and then back to Hilary's for a Christmas dinner and then we all sat around on the cushions on the floor drinking wine and listening to Fleetwood Mac and Pink Floyd. We all got a little drunk, and then I noticed that Jan and Malcolm were kissing and cuddling together. Hilary then led me by the hand upstairs and into the bedroom and started kissing me and telling me she loved me. It was all very confusing. Try as I might I couldn't get the picture of Jan and Malcolm out of my head. Hilary told me not to worry and that she was mine for the night and pulled me down onto the bed, but even if I wanted to, I couldn't have performed. My head was all over the place and I just said I couldn't, not with Jan and Malcolm just downstairs. She told me not to be so silly and what did I think that they were doing. She said that Malcolm had told her that Jan was crazy about him and that he really loved her. Hilary didn't mind as she had fallen in love with me and just wanted to be with me and for me to make love to her. It wouldn't affect anything, we could still all be together and live our lives as before, she insisted, we would all be sharing and caring with people who loved us. I said that it was all too soon - I was unprepared for what was happening. I thought the world of her and I loved being with her but I had never thought of anything like this. I was sorry to spoil everything but I needed time to think and I just wanted for Jan and me to go home. I then made my way downstairs and into the darkness. I called for Jan and said that I was sorry but I think that we ought to go home. I could hear the rustling in the darkness and I tried to close my mind to what might be happening and then I felt Jan at my side saying "Ok Ronnie don't worry I'm here. If you really want to go that's fine. I'll get our coats". Hilary had followed me down the stairs and through the gloom cast by the kitchen light that Jan had put on; I saw her shrug at Malcolm, and her face looked despondent. I turned to them both and said that I was very sorry and that I didn't want to hurt anyone and maybe would see everything differently when my head had cleared. I then went over to Hilary, hugged her, and said, "No hard feelings", and as I turned to shake Malcolm's hand I said, "I suppose that was part of the problem". Once out and in the car Jan and I were silent for a while, and then Jan said, "It's only a bit of fun you know, it doesn't affect the way I feel about you. You're taking everything so seriously, why can't you just join in the fun. It really doesn't mean anything – it's just a little escape from the humdrum ordinariness of my life. But if you don't want to join in then I will do nothing. I don't want to hurt you"? Now I really was confused. I was the dog in the manger, the one spoiling everyone else's fun? Why was I making such a big deal of it and ruining that little bit of escapism for Jan. She had always been the loyal wife, staying at home looking after the children, while I had charged around fulfilling my own whims. Maybe this was payback time and she felt I should just let her have her fun. As long as she came back to me, and it seems she was giving me license to take Hilary as compensation, (so that she wouldn't feel guilty), why was that a problem? I was in shock that things had got this far, and felt this was a very dangerous game to be playing.

CHAPTER 8

A FAMILY CHRISTMAS

Our first Christmas in St. Agnes was lovely – just looking up at the village with all the coloured lights was magical in itself and inside our house it was decked throughout with tinsel and streamers and two Christmas trees. It started with Adam and Simon's birthday party and then all the boys were invited to various Christmas parties and they really enjoyed themselves. On Christmas Eve from our window we could hear the band and the carol singers up the village and once all the boys had gone to bed Jan and I set about wrapping up their presents. As per our usual tradition I crept into their bedrooms with pillowcases full of their presents and then joined Jan in bed. Like every other Christmas we were awoken at about 4 a.m. with a rustling and giggling from Adam & Simon's bedroom and I called out to them to get back to sleep and then again a couple of hours later with the same response. Finally at 7 a.m. Jan went down to put the turkey in the oven while I made a cup of tea and then the bedroom was invaded by all four boys with their pillowcases to open up their presents with us. As usual Mark just ripped open everything in five minutes scattering paper everywhere whilst Troy opened each present carefully and played with it for a few minutes before going on to the next. Meanwhile Adam and Simon were comparing parcels to try to ensure they both opened similar ones as they usually got the same presents unless it was a big one to share. Then after a light breakfast of home cooked sausage rolls we all went for a short walk while the dinner cooked. The afternoon was spent playing games and then it was time for high tea followed by sitting watching the television whilst blowing our stomachs out further with chocolates, nuts and crisps until it was time to stagger off to bed totally bloated. Next day it was all out for the Boxing Day walk and back for a cold collage of left-overs. Gradually over the years the Christmas traditions extended but the central chore of Christmas Day and Boxing Day stayed just as it had done when we all first became a family. New Year's Eve we met Malcolm and Hilary with their friends in the old Star pub in Truro and then we seemed to end up in the flat of a guy from the Canary Islands with his girlfriend who were both nurses at the local hospital, along with a crowd of others. They were all falling about with laughter and smoking pot and listening to an LP of Pete & Dud's uncensored show (Peter Cook and Dudley Moore) which to me sounded no more than a continual stream of expletives. Jan and I slipped quietly away and home.

CHAPTER 9

FINDING STAFF FOR DEBENHAMS

The first week of the New Year Jan and I and the boys went up to Plymouth with Malcolm and Hilary. We all went to Debenhams first to meet the manager who showed us where we were to construct our counters and then Jan and Hilary took the children off shopping to spend their Christmas money in the sales, while Malcolm and I started measuring up and designing the counter. Then we all met up to make our way back, stopping at a pub on the way for a meal. Next, we had to sort out an advert for girls to run the in-store shop. We agreed that Hilary should do the first interviews and when she had whittled down the applicants I would help decide on the successful candidate. We decided we would need one senior girl and a junior to cover for lunch and coffee breaks and in case we were lucky enough for it to get really busy. Malcolm reckoned that it would take him no more than two days to construct the counter and Hilary said that she would ask the manager if we could borrow one of their rooms to hold interviews for the prospective sales personnel. She would hold the first interviews on the first day that Malcolm was working on the counter, and then on the second day, thus sorting out both the counter and the staff in the two days. Jan and I only needed to go up the second day which would be fine, as the boys were back at school and we only needed to take Adam and Simon.

The interviews for the senior girl went well and although Hilary had narrowed it down to three, there was one girl who was head and shoulders above all the others. Her name was Janet and she was a pleasantly attractive girl in her early thirties. She seemed intelligent and capable and was very interested in colour and design. Hilary and I agreed that she should work with Janet for the first couple of weeks to show her the ropes and I would look after the Truro shop but would go to Plymouth on the Monday to see how they were getting on. We also had to see the manager to go through the procedures and work out an advertising program. Finding a suitable junior was a little more difficult as none of them seemed that bright or interested in the job itself, only as a way of earning money. Malcolm had made a superb job of the counters and all that was left was to dress them and fill them with books. Malcolm also said that, while I was up in Plymouth, he would take Jan out for a car ride and a drink; she needed a break he thought. I couldn't really argue.

***

Then, at the end of January Adam caught a bad cold that seemed to induce a really bad asthma attack. I grew up prone to asthma as did Troy, so we owned the necessary spin-halers, and at first we just took the usual precautions as before but he seemed to get no better. His breathing became more and more laboured and by morning we were really worried. We called the doctor and Jan cuddled Adam in a blanket. When the doctor came he said Adam had contracted double pneumonia and the situation was grave. He called an ambulance and Adam was rushed to hospital and placed in intensive care. We both were desperately worried and Jan seemed to think it was some retribution for what had happened over Christmas. We visited him every day and slowly he got better and after a fortnight we were able to take him home. He rapidly recovered after that and was soon back to normal but it had given us a scare.

***

Meanwhile at Debenhams it only took a couple of months to prove our idea successful. We finally got a junior, Anne, to work with Janet and I arranged for all four of us Malcolm, Hilary, Jan and me to go up every Friday to assess the week's business and take the figures and see what money was to come back filtered through Debenhams. Business was booming and I think that even the Plymouth manager was taken by surprise, so much so that I was summoned up to London again to see the directors about extending the franchise. In the meantime I had met again with Keith Turner and he had arranged a loan for us of £10,000 through the solicitors Parnell Chegwyn, so it was with confidence that I agreed to do Exeter, Taunton, Bath, Bristol and Swindon and thereafter they wanted the whole 78 stores to be involved by the end of 1979.

***

I took Jan, Malcolm and Hilary with the children up to my parent's house in St. Albans. It was Easter and the children were going to stay with them for the Easter break and then they were going to bring them down to St. Agnes and would stay on for an extended holiday in our caravan. My sister had just gone to America where her husband had a new job, this was the day before emails etc., and we pretty much lost touch with each other for many years.

***

I had known what the meeting with Debenhams was to entail from the preliminary phone call, hence our en masse visit to St. Albans so that the four of us could wend our way slowly back through the towns where we were to do business to meet the managers and interview prospective staff. We had fun looking around the sights of the respective towns and staying in bed and breakfast, interviewing girls, meeting the managers and organising the counters. We all got on well together, although I was still uneasy at the way Jan and Malcolm seemed to be drawing closer together, and the way Hilary never missed an opportunity to demonstrate how available she was for me. My ego was flattered, especially as Jan was still just as loving towards me, but I couldn't make the pieces fit in my head and I had a constant fear of where it was all going.

CHAPTER 10

JAN WAS ENJOYING LIFE/I LEARNED MY LESSON

Again I was neglecting Jan but she now had Malcolm to amuse her and I was becoming aggravated by Hillary constantly telling me how happy Jan and Malcolm were together. Then she really alarmed me by telling me that Malcolm had fallen in love with Jan, and she believed, from what Malcolm told her, that Jan had also fallen in love with Malcolm. With these insidious whispers in my ear and seeing how happy Jan was, I turned to Hillary for comfort. While my mum and dad had been looking after the children, first at St. Albans and then in St. Agnes we had been going out to parties and weekends at their friends' homes and I especially remember one at Malcolm's friend Pete and Cath's house. The entire usual crowd was there and as always as the night wore on the joints started to be passed around. At these functions I always ended up the sober one. I was lucky drink minimally affected me and I never really got drunk. Besides I had to be there to look after Jan and get her home. However, on this occasion they all seemed to conspire to make sure I loosened up. When a big fat joint was passed to me I took a drag and tried to pass it back but no-one would take it. I took another drag and again offered it on but again it was declined. I ended up almost finishing it and then I felt as sick as a dog. I went outside but could not stop retching. My head was clear and I knew all that was happening but I felt so ill and I was doubled up. Jan had never seen me like that before. It was usually me taking care of her and she was really worried. There I was standing over a drain outside doubled over and unable to control the continual spasmodic convulsions. As I sank down exhausted I feebly asked her if she could drive us home and she helped me to the car and into the passenger seat. It was only afterwards I realised how worried she must have been. She had been drinking and she would never normally have contemplated such a drive but she asked me if she should take me to the hospital but I insisted that we just go home and not to worry, once I could rest I would soon be better. So she drove me back and somehow I staggered into the house and collapsed on the bed. In the morning, apart from a very sore stomach and a splitting headache I was alright but I would never touch anything like that again.

***

Our success grew more and more now, and we added responsibility of the other Debenhams shops. As I had to make regular visits I decided to invest in a motor caravan. I had seen a converted Leyland ambulance offered for sale at £2,000 on the outskirts of Redruth so I went over to take a look. It seemed ideal, it even had its own shower and portaloo and could sleep four comfortably and with the children sharing we could possibly squeeze all six of us in. I had visions of Jan and me with the four children hitting the road and stopping overnight in leafy glades miles into the country. In the school holidays they could all come with me to visit the various Debenhams shops and we could extend it to a few days holiday. To me it spelt freedom but Jan wasn't too keen as she said that we didn't know how reliable it was and with my luck she could see us breaking down in all these remote places. She said that it would be far better to wait a little while and get a new one when we could afford it. But impetuous as ever and against her advice I bought it.

***

To try to show her how much fun we could all have I decided to take the family including Jan's mum and dad to Gorran Haven a little seaside cove in the Roseland Peninsular. We would make an early start and take bacon and sausages and tea and drinks for the Adam and Simon and cook breakfast when we got there and spend a day on the beach. After a week of rain the weather was finally turning and the weather forecast for the day was good. When we arrived at Gorran Haven I parked the motor caravan away from everyone else in the bottom corner of the field and we all sat round to a nice breakfast. We had brought chairs for Jan's mum and dad so we all made our way down to the beach. It was a lovely hot day and everyone enjoyed themselves. We could pop back to the 'van for tea and then wander back to the beach and I could see Jan beginning to think that it might have been a good idea. At the end of the day we all wended our way back to the motor caravan, tired and ready to go home. Then as I tried to drive away the wheels just spun in the wet grass and I realised that the bottom of the field hadn't dried out. It was an automatic and I could only use the lowest gear setting but the weight of the motor caravan just dug it deeper and deeper into the mud. We tried putting the towels under the wheels to try to give it some grip but that only resulted in them becoming buried in thick mud. Some people came to try to help us to push it out while I tried to slowly drive it but it was no use, it just seemed to get deeper and deeper and those kind souls who came to help just got splattered in mud. After about two hours I was beginning to despair. The children were tired and hungry and Jan's mum and dad were completely fed up. Jan said that she should have known something would go wrong and how was I going to get them out of this mess. To get a taxi back would have cost a fortune even if I could have found one to take us and I would still be left with the problem of what to do with the motor caravan. Just then one of the locals who had been watching us came over carrying a roll of old carpet. Between us we stuck it under the wheels and slowly they started to grip and the motor caravan began to move. With much slipping and sliding I finally got it onto the road and rushed back to show my grateful thanks to the kind man who had helped us and I gave him my last £10 for his trouble. We then drove home in silence, our first venture had not been a success and I knew it would be a while before I could persuade Jan to risk it again.

CHAPTER 11

JAN & I /TIME TO RECAPTURE ROMANCE

When we finally got back to St. Agnes the weather was one of those hot Spring days and when we woke up the next morning it was the same. I wanted to escape from Malcolm and Hilary and the children were still with my mum and dad so I suggested that Jan and I spent a day together, just ourselves, away from everyone. We packed a picnic and drove to the Roseland Peninsular. After driving down a wooded valley we parked the car and walked eventually arriving at the coast path. There just past Carne beach we found a small deserted cove that looked so beautiful it was just made for us. We lazed the day away having our picnic, going in the water for a swim and making love on the beach. The only slightly disturbing thing was that when I looked up from our embrace I thought I saw divers in the water but on reflection maybe they were just seals. To both of us it had been our perfect day and although we were to have many more, that one was special. We watched the sun go down and then stopped at an old country inn for a meal on our way home. Nothing had gone wrong, nothing had spoilt the day and that night I felt more close to Jan than I had for a long time. Why couldn't it always be like that? Why was I constantly involving myself in so many things, chasing elusive dreams when all I really wanted to do, was spend my days with Jan and the family to the exclusion of everything else. But the reality was that each time I thought that I could get enough money to walk away and live that dream, it never seemed to work out that way. Perhaps I should realize dreams were just that, and maybe I could make my own world with Jan and the boys, it would be just a simple but beautiful life that didn't need money.
***

The problem was, when I saw an opportunity or an opportunity was before me, it was almost a compulsion to try to see what I could do with it, and so it happened, one day when I met the creepy and obnoxious Mr. Wellings from whom I had got my first Truro shop, he was also an employee of the Independent newspaper and handled our advertising. He told me about two other potential shop premises becoming available with a much larger display area and actual glass instead of brick windows. One was in Ferris Town on the road leading to Truro station and was the cheaper of the two and the other was in Pydar Street, nearer the centre. As the Truro shop was to be the hub of the Debenhams franchise, I felt we needed more impressive premises.

The choice for me was clinched when I found out a new large Tesco store was to open almost opposite the Pydar Street shop. It would be the main Tesco outlet in Cornwall, the only other one being the small shop in Falmouth. The shop itself had a large double frontage and a further two floors above. It also had a large rear garden with a huge shed stretching through to the Leats (a cul-de-sac serving the rear of the premises in High Cross and River Street). Although the rent was higher, there was so much room I immediately thought about sub-letting to offset the rent. I asked both John Wellings and Keith Turner if they knew of other people looking for premises in the centre of Truro. Keith came up with a furrier, Charles Farkas, who made and repaired fur coats who wanted a display window and a workroom. After meeting with him, I gave him one of the large display windows and one of the two rooms at the back as a workshop. His wife Joan said that she would be more than happy to work out front with Hilary looking after her husband's clients but also helping Hilary with our Design shop. I reflected her assistance in the rent and everyone was happy.
***
Secondly John Wellings was a model railway enthusiast and the group he belonged two had always wanted to do a model railway exhibition, so I said that they could rent the

large shed at the back to house for their exhibition which could be accessed by a side entrance. They would recoup the costs of their display, which was also a labour of love by charging an entrance fee to see it. There was also a small area at the back that had been the small kitchen for the premises and I thought of the idea of turning this into a sandwich and refreshment bar for people visiting the exhibition and generally shopping in that area of Truro. A small courtyard adjacent to the shed housing the model railway display and alongside the kitchen would make an ideal sitting out area once it had been smartened up and with a few café tables and chairs. Hillary happened to know a woman who used to run a small café in Truro but had lost her premises when rents increased. She was a lovely woman and immediately took to making the little area her pride and joy. Moving forward, then Hillary suggested on the first floor we open a second-hand clothes outlet. There was only one other on the outskirts of Truro and it was very successful. Joan Farkas was also very keen on the idea and she said that she and Hillary could run it between them and they would vet all the clothes that came in to make sure that we only took quality items. The owner of the clothes could display them on our racks for two months. Prices would be mutually agreed between Hillary or Joan and the owner and the proceeds of sale split 60% to the owner and 40% to us. Any item that hadn't sold after two months could be taken back by the owner. The outlet was to be called 'Whirligig' a play on the word roundabout illustrating the turnaround of the clothes. Finally the top floor was let to an upholsterer and curtain maker that fitted in nicely with our design outlet. From the rents from the various different occupiers I actually was making roughly double what I was paying in rent and everything was up and ready for the summer of 1978. We were doing well.

CHAPTER 12

IT'S COMPLICATED

The Truro shop was making a profit, even if we didn't seek to advertise there, we were doing quite well. The second hand clothes shop after the initial advertising also did well and the model railway and sandwich and refreshment bar were doing a roaring summer trade. The only slight fly in the ointment came later when the upholsterer turned out to be an alcoholic and became completely unreliable, disappearing for days on end and leaving our orders uncompleted. Apart from that the Debenhams outlets were going from strength to strength and starting to show profit above their running costs, although initially any surplus money went into opening and kitting out another store. We used Plymouth as our flagship and tested out any new sales ideas there before introducing them to the other stores and initially Malcolm, Hillary, Jan and I would visit there every Friday. I would then be responsible for visiting the other stores.

***

Then just to complicate things the Opel failed its MOT and I was stuck without a car. Keith Turner had rung me to check how things were going and he told me of a car that I could have for nothing if I could just pick it up and it would do to tie me over until I could sort out another car. It was an Austin 1100 and needed to be picked up from Crawley in Sussex some 350 miles away. If I could go in a couple of days' time I could get a free lift to London and make my way down from there. I thought that it would be worth collecting just to give me transport until all the commissions were paid out and then just maybe I could get my dream car. My lift up to London was in a pantechnicon and I was squashed in the front with two burly removal men. They were pleasant enough but in the seven hour journey conversation was limited and their choice of deafening music wasn't my taste, but at least it was free. They kindly dropped me off at Lewisham and I was able to catch a train to Crawley. There I phoned the number Keith had given me for the owner of the car. He told me which bus to catch and ten hours after I left my house at 8.30 a.m. I was walking up his drive. Then I saw why the car was free, it was mustard and rust coloured and at first sight I wasn't sure whether it would make the journey back. I thought that I had better start straight away and filling it up with petrol, I was on my way and surprisingly driving at a steady pace I reached the A30 in two hours. Then on a remote stretch of road the engine died. I waited and after half an hour it started up again, the same thing happened three more times and I eventually got back just before4 a.m. When I took it to the garage the next day it was a fault with the fuel line and then when they checked over everything else they said that it would almost certainly fail its next MOT and to fix it would be more than the car was worth. When I told Keith a couple of weeks later he said that he was sorry but he wanted to contact me as he had just seen a Triumph Stag he wanted to buy and would I be interested in buying his Audi 100L from him as he could fix the finance for me. It was a lovely car with an automatic gearbox and a brilliant HiFi system in it that Keith had put in himself to his order. Also being Keith's car it was in immaculate order as he was a bit of a car fanatic. I jumped at the idea and Keith duly sorted out the paperwork and I became the proud owner.

CHAPTER 13

DEBENHAMS DEMANDING MORE ATTENTION/& SO DID HILARY

A couple of weeks later I had a call from Debenhams saying that one of the girls in Swindon had handed in her notice and had to be replaced. They also asked me to look over their branch in Reading and talk to the manager there about the possibility of making that our next branch to be opened. I originally thought that the four of us could go, me, Jan, Malcolm and Hillary but Malcolm was working on a cottage in Trevellas which he said he needed to finish and anyway he said that he wouldn't really be needed until any work had to be done. Jan said that she didn't want to leave the children and it was suggested that just Hillary and I should go. Hillary wanted to take the motor caravan, she had friends who lived in Newbury and she would love to see them and perhaps we could spend the first night there and then if we were kept late in Swindon we could break our journey camping on Salisbury Plain and then drive straight back. She wanted to go on the Sunday as that was her friend's birthday and we could do Reading the next morning and interview girls in Swindon in the afternoon. If she notified the local employment agency immediately they could arrange for the candidates to be available. I said that I would rather take the car and we could come back that night and it would only mean one night away. However the situation decided itself when I noticed that the MOT on the Audi had run out and the garage couldn't fit us in until the following week. The only transport left was the motor caravan and that was a slow lumbering old bus so the chance of getting back at a reasonable hour on the Monday night was unlikely.
***

We arrived at Hillary's friends at teatime on Sunday and to my slight consternation Hillary introduced me as her boyfriend. They had made up a double bed for us in the lounge and we were to have dinner at eight. We sat around and Hillary seemed to be in her element cosying up to me on the settee and then her friend asked when we were going to get married. Hillary hugged me and said we hadn't set a date yet but as soon as the business was able to spare us. Then I realised that I was part of some sort of fantasy game of Hillary's and I was expected to play along. Again everything was wrong. I didn't want to be there and my shyness and confusion was making me tongue-tied. I thought that her friends must be thinking of me as some sort of idiot but I just wanted to be out of that situation and then I thought of that double bed and what Hillary was expecting of me. I wanted to be back with Jan and I hated the game Hilary was playing... I suddenly said that I felt ill and that I had terrible stomach pains. Hillary's friends suggested I go and lay down in the bed and I was pleased to get away, just to be by myself. A little later Hillary came in and kissed my forehead and asked how I felt. I told her that I still felt terrible and I was really sorry, I didn't want to spoil her evening. I told her that I wouldn't be able to eat anything and that it would be better if she left me to join her friends. She came in one more time to give me some medicine, for which I thanked her and then I said that I would try to sleep, she had come all this way to see her friends and that she mustn't disappoint them. At about 1a.m I felt her creep into bed. She was a little the worse for drink and she cuddled up to me, but I feigned sleep. The next morning I made my apologies to everyone concerned, feeling extremely embarrassed, and said that I was feeling better but I was sorry to have missed their company.

***

Hillary and I met the Reading manager and explained to him our operation. We were able to give him figures for the Plymouth shop that had the longest track record and he was impressed. He invited us to lunch and over lunch he asked when we would be able to get our counter up and running. I was a little concerned that we were already over extended and I told him that we would prefer not to do his shop as a one off but to include him in the group of stores that we would be fitting out next year as it made more economic sense to us. He was disappointed and said that he had hoped that we would be talking of no more than a couple of months and couldn't we bring a group of stores forward to do together as he had been told that the whole seventy-eight were supposed to be up and running by the end of next year. I said that we would look into it. Next we went on to Swindon where Hillary had narrowed the applications down to five and we had been allocated an interview room at the job centre. First we had to show our face at the Swindon store where the manager told us that he was very pleased with the way things were going and insisted on showing us round. By the time we had completed our interviews and chosen the girl to fulfil the vacancy it was coming up to 8.30 p.m. I said that we should start to strike for home and see how far we could get but Hillary wanted to camp the night near Knighton Down on Salisbury Plain. She then said that she knew that I was still thinking of Jan but what did I think that Malcolm and Jan had been up to while we were away. She said that they had contrived things so that they could be together and that we should make the most of it, why should they have all the fun. Suddenly I felt annoyed and in the need of some compensation for being manoeuvred out of the way. I agreed and that night Hillary and I slept together. When I got back I told Jan how I had been ill on the Sunday night and asked what she and Malcolm had been up to. She looked astonished. She said that she hadn't seen him. Colin, Jan's brother, had phoned to say that he and Sally might split up and her mum and dad were very upset as they were very fond of Sally. So on Sunday night she and the children had all had dinner with her mum and dad and stayed in their apartment to watch television. On Monday Malcolm had phoned to ask if she would meet him for a drink but she had been working all day getting the house tidy and didn't feel like going out. Besides she would have needed to ask her mother to look after the children and she was upset enough so she had stayed with her. I felt very guilty and I realised that I had taken too much notice of the poison Hillary was feeding me.

***

The success of the business was slowly being tarnished for me by what was happening in our personal lives. Jan was still being the perfect mother with the children and had a lightness and happiness about her that I hadn't seen for a long time. I didn't want to spoil it for her, but I was still worried that she seemed to becoming obsessed with Malcolm, was all that Hillary had said true? I had always felt very comfortable in our marriage, was Jan teaching me a lesson? Meanwhile, Hillary was stepping up our involvement, wanting me to set up house with her and suggesting that we leave Jan and Malcolm to be happy together and she would be everything I ever wanted, but it wasn't what I wanted... Somehow, I needed to know what it was all about. When I tentatively tried to broach the subject with Jan, I mentioned how happy she seemed lately. She surprised me by saying "of course I am happy, I have two wonderful men in love with me and that would make any woman happy". I wasn't to be so heavy about everything she added. I couldn't fault how loving and affectionate she was to me, so why couldn't I feel the same way, with two lovely women in love with me. I wondered if it was just jealousy on my part seeing someone else able to make Jan feel that way. I was chasing around here, there and everywhere again, whereas Malcolm was always there paying her attention and making her feel special. I tried, and the moments we were together she knew I loved her, but I always had these self-inflicted pressures getting in the way. Jan's happiness was paramount to me, but eventually I knew that I had to face the situation head on, I didn't see it as just a game.

***

If all Hillary said was true, then I would let Jan go, and maybe end up with Hillary, if that was how it was to be I decided, but I couldn't believe this was happening to us and it was not what I wanted. Then, I returned to the house one day, and found Jan was upstairs looking out of the window at Malcolm's little yellow van parked at the top of the hill. Clearly, she was absolutely obsessed with him

***

So that night, I told Jan we had to talk, and then shared with her all that Hillary had told me, that she and Malcolm were in love with each other. I went on to say, if that was true, I wouldn't stand in her way, I would agree to any arrangement she wanted, but I would have to leave, because I was not prepared to share her. Jan was dumbfounded. She had no idea how I felt and thought we were just having fun. She admitted Malcolm made her feel good, now she felt like more than just a housewife and mum, but she loved me and couldn't think of life without me. I was everything she wanted, not Malcolm. It was just fun with him, and she hated his idea of sex, that had really put her off, but the rest of it was like a drug, an adrenaline rush that somebody other than her husband could think that she was so special and profess to love her. She enjoyed the flirtation, but never wanted it to go any further and after the initial encounter; she had tried to keep him at arm's length. But now she knew how unhappy it was making me, she didn't want it to continue, although she said that it would be hard for her, as it would be like coming off drugs. Not because it was Malcolm, but because of the high adoration from someone else, it made her happy and excited. In fact, she explained that all this made her feel like a teenager again and that was going to be hard to lose. I apologised and said I only wished I didn't feel that way, but she hugged me and said she understood and that I had been amazing, however, it had to come to an end sometime and I would always be the only person that ever mattered to her, and she was sorry that she had hurt me. What a relief, I felt; things had almost gone too far.

***

Things were still going to be difficult as I still had to work with Hillary and technically Malcolm was still a partner, but that at least was solved, as when Jan told him that she felt things had got out of hand and that she just wanted to be a good wife to me, he ran off in his van leaving both Jan and Hillary, and never contacted us again. Hillary was now heart-broken. She knew I wouldn't leave Jan and now she had lost Malcolm. When she got home and found his things gone, she phoned me, sobbing and crying, and Jan said that I ought to go and fetch her. So I did, and took her home. She joined us for dinner and then when she was all cried out, I put her to bed, in our bed. Later that night, I found myself sleeping in the bed with two women, Jan and Hillary, but Jan made sure that she was in the middle. After a couple of nights I took Hillary home and I explained that we would continue to work together, and I still felt the world of her, but Jan and the children came first, although she would always be my best friend. She said that she understood and she knew in her heart that I would never leave Jan, and that was why she was so upset when she lost Malcolm as well. I obviously had ruined everything for them, but I was glad that I had.

CHAPTER 14

I GRABBED THE LADDER, BUT SNAKES WERE LOOMING.

While all this was going on the landlady of our Truro shop who owned the dairy a few doors up told me she wanted to sell it, but I wasn't to worry as my lease covered me for three years and there a little of two years remained. But I found out Pydar Street, with the new Tesco's up and running and other chains looking at property there, was soon going to be a very expensive area. So I suggested if she was prepared to accept a structured deal I would buy it from her. We agreed on a purchase price of £60,000 to be paid in four twelve month installments of £15,000, completing the purchase in three years. It was a bargain and I could just about raise the first installment. It was a gamble but business was good and I was confident in twelve months' time I would be ready with the second. I discussed it with Keith Turner and he said that he would have no trouble underwriting it for me and that I had got a bargain. We instructed solicitors to proceed. When John Wellings came round to sort out our next adverts I told him that I was buying the shop and that I could give him a more secure lease for his railway exhibition. He asked me how I could afford it and that I should have gone through him as he was the agent for the landlady and that's how he found the premises for us in the first place. I apologised and said that it had just come about during my discussions with her when she told me she was selling up. He said that he would have a chat with her as he should be earning a commission.

***

The next thing I heard was that she would not be proceeding with me as she had received a better offer. I went to see her and she told me that John Welling's visited her enquiring about the property. He then came back a few days later with a Mr. Angilley who offered her a similar structured deal but with a purchase price of £80,000 and four payments of £20,000 over four years and he offered her the first £20,000 as an upfront deposit pending completion of sale. I expressed my extreme disappointed, as I thought we already shook hands on the deal, but she said Mr. Wellings advised her I was a man of straw, and hadn't got the money and could well renege on the deal, whereas Mr. Angilley offered all the necessary bank references. I was furious and immediately phoned John Wellings to ask why he shafted me. He just said the landlady was his client and protection of her interests was paramount. He thought Mr. Angilley held more collateral than I, and besides he already conducted other deals with him. I said it poorly excused poaching my idea and rubbishing me to the landlady, to which he replied pompously, that business was for grown-ups, and I shouldn't try to run with the big boys. I just slammed the phone down. I still had two and a half years left on the lease, but I was under no illusions I would be looking for new premises when the lease was up.

***

In addition to running the shops we also got involved in doing some of the decoration work for clients. Jan and I became a pretty good wallpapering team and with the lessons I had learnt from old Alfred we became quite expert. We even put Hessian wall covering up in Keith Turners house in Truro while he constantly plied us with great big glasses of wine. Even in that inebriated state we did a first class job, so much so that he got us to decorate the top floor of his house in Fowey when he got back with his wife Avril after they had been apart for two years. There was only one occasion when I was a little worried and that was when we had to hang an expensive silk wall covering in a ladies lounge and, despite all Alfred's tips a small amount of glue seeped out under the wall light. It couldn't have been in a worst place with the light shining full on it and the amount of wall covering supplied had been exact. To replace the strip would have meant ordering another roll at an exorbitant cost. Try as I might I couldn't remove the mark and in the end I had to leave it and hope. I couldn't understand how when the women saw the finished room she was delighted and then I saw that standing away from it the wall light cast a shadow just where the slight mark was. One of the strangest jobs I had was pasting a rubberised wall fabric under the trade name Gallon onto the walls and ceiling of a concrete barge moored down at Gweek. They were to use the barge on a forthcoming round-the-world trip and I was pasting the fabric straight onto the concrete walls to give it a softer finish and provide insulation for warmth and sound. It took me ages often working in very cramped conditions and with Jan's help on the longer stretches. Anyway we finally finished it and the boat was mentioned on the local news and they even commented on the rubberised interior. I never knew what happened to the boat afterwards.

***

Although business was going well, the cost of opening the Debenhams shops still meant that I was trading on overdraft and this was exacerbated by the long delay in getting our money from Debenhams. When I first negotiated the borrowing, interest rates were at 8% and I was being charged 4% over base that is I was paying 12%. Most of my suppliers gave me a 40% discount and 40% of that went to Debenhams leaving me with 24% total so 12% surplus covered the running costs of the business with a small surplus to start paying back the set up costs. However, each time a new shop opened, the set up costs increased. Also most of my suppliers were small businesses who insisted on strict adherence to the 30 day credit allowance. As I had to wait anything up to two months to get my money from Debenhams, I had to carry the difference between my settlement and reimbursement from Debenhams and the more I sold the larger the deficit I had to carry albeit for a month. But as business was going up in a steep curve it would be a while before I had accumulated enough from my surplus to cover the deficit. Then interest rates started to rise, slowly at first and by the end of my first trading year they stood at 11.75% making my borrowing costs 15.75%, already I was trying to carry everything on little over an 8% margin. Theoretically all those 8% spread throughout the stores would eventually add up to a considerable surplus but the smaller the margin the longer it would take. Then it started to become critical. By October 1979 interest rates were 15% and I was paying 19% and I was only just able to cover the wages. It was becoming more and more difficult and then disaster struck. From the beginning of 1980 to April 1980 they escalated alarmingly peaking at 20%. Now I was losing money and the more business I did the more money I was losing as the bigger deficit I had to carry. With eight stores now operating my position was untenable and Debenhams were pressurizing me to do the other seventy. In my desperation during 1979 I had become involved in a brokerage business to try to subsidise the Debenhams operation and to provide sufficient surplus to open the other stores and it looked as if I might just pull it off.

CHAPTER 15

ANOTHER OPPORTUNITY

I was in Keith Turners office just before Christmas1978 bemoaning the increasing interest charges and explaining how tight everything was becoming. I said that I needed a secondary source of income to prop up the Debenhams business and to try to generate enough money not to have to borrow so heavily. He said that it was a coincidence because he had been talking about me to one of his clients, Chris Cullum, who runs a brokerage business as well as other businesses involving the American bases in Europe. He was shortly going to be travelling extensively around the German bases and wanted somebody to look after the brokerage on a joint commission basis. Keith had talked about me and Chris Cullum said that I sounded the perfect sort of person if Keith could get me. Keith had said that he would ask, but he knew that I was very busy on the Debenhams franchise. However, if I could cope with both, there was a chance to make good money. A meeting was arranged with Chris Cullum at his house in St. Austell and Keith came along to introduce me. He was similar in many ways to Keith, but a lot harder and coarser. He was equally tall and stocky with a beard but his hair was thinner than Keith's and veering towards baldness. On the way over Keith had explained that he had been on a business trip with him to Germany, and while he was pleasant fellow most of the time, he had a vile temper and very dangerous mood swings. He put this down to a metal plate that he had in his skull after a terrible accident that also caused some brain damage. However, to me Chris Cullum was charm itself, welcoming me like some long lost friend, and the welcome from his wife, Liz, was even warmer. He said that Keith had told him all about me and he had great admiration for my business ideas and said I was just the sort of intuitive fellow he would like to work with. His wife said that I must take Jan and the children round to tea on Sunday as she would like to get to know us all. Liz was the spitting image of Shirley Williams the SDP politician; in fact in my head I could never separate the two.

***

Chris said he was happy to pass everything over to me and I could use his house as a base while he was away. He gave me all his files to go back with and said that if I came round on the following Monday, after I had read the files, we could go through everything. He hoped that I would take up Liz's invitation for tea with the family, but that would be a social occasion and not to discuss business. He then explained that he and Liz worked together on a heraldry business for the American soldiers. Basically it consisted of tracing the origins of their names and working out heraldic signs to complement the name, with a brief potted history of where their name had come from. Liz, who was an artist, would then design a large plaque incorporating the name and a lot of heraldic motifs for them to hang on the wall. The American people love to feel that they are part of history they explained. Apparently, they were willing to pay handsomely for the scroll and plaque they were given, (although what Liz and Chris had cobbled together didn't bear too much scrutiny in my opinion).

***

We accepted the invitation to tea and we all turned up with the children on the Sunday, as invited. Liz was the perfect hostess and served sandwiches and cakes, with tea and soft drinks for the boys all served up on beautiful Willow patterned china. In our conversation it transpired that Chris had been in the army based in Germany and Liz was the daughter of a wealthy broker in the City who lived in Corsham, Wilshire. It was her family connections that had allowed Chris to get started on his brokerage and ancestry business, and it seems it was her money that was the solid base. The house was a large, rambling late Victorian property with a terraced garden and a swimming pool that was covered for the winter. The boys were very impressed and were given the guided tour. They were on their best behaviour and Liz said that they were angels. I mentioned that we were all going up to London in the New Year and the boys were really looking forward to it. Liz casually mentioned that she had a house just at the back of Harrods, it happened to be empty at the moment. It belonged to her family, but we were welcome to use it and stay there when we went up in the New Year. It seemed a fantastic opportunity being right in the centre of Knightsbridge and the boys couldn't believe their luck. When we went there it was a beautiful little period house situated immediately behind Harrods in Walton Place, and was filled with antiques. It seemed to be an enormous amount of trust to give us the free run of it, but we behaved ourselves impeccably, so much so that Liz said that we could use it anytime.

***

Meanwhile, I was suddenly plunged into the brokerage world buying and selling everything from gold, silver and copper, U.S.Dollars and barrels of oil, selling spot or futures in vast quantities on minute margins. I was dealing with new people such as in Joel Block in Germany, Bill Meymood in the Gulf States, Vieten Rayan in Saudi Arabia, Leon Valdez in Venezuela, Admiral Corcoran in Canada and Jim MacAvinia and Elliott Baron in the United States. It was in the days before faxes and e-mails and apart from the telephone the only other means of communication was through a telex machine that punched your message out in a series of holes in a long reel of paper. You then dialed your number abroad and when you received the signal you fed your long string of paper into the telex machine and it printed out your message on a reel of paper on the telex machine at the other end. It was a fraction of the cost of a phone call and as I already spent a lot contacting and talking to these people at all different times of day and night due to the varying time zones, I decided to get a telex machine installed in my garage with a bell up in the house to let me know when a telex was coming through. Chris and Liz already went over to the continent leaving me detailed instructions where to contact them and where to pay in any cheques should they arrive and a contact number for Liz's father should I need any help although he was soon to be going off to Spain. As backup I was given the address and phone number of Liz's brother a lecturer at Glasgow Poly who lived in Buchlyvie, Stirlingshire, Scotland who was also instructed to help me should I require it in her father's absence. Also they gave me the address of Liz's sister in Florence should I need any money and they intended to end up there.

***

I was to visit their house in St. Austell to collect the post a couple of times a week but they also had a live in lodger there, Robbie, who was looking after the ancestry business and enquiries for them. He was a typical Scot tall and thin, with a shock of curly ginger hair and a ginger beard. He was a nice chap and I got on well with him although, Liz had warned me that he had a temper. There were also all sorts of other people dropping round the house. I had noticed some of them when Chris and Liz were there, but now they had left, it seemed they would all go in and treat it as if it were their own. One of them, who I got on very well with was Glyn Morris, he turned up regularly with his girlfriend Tamsin. He was a graphic designer and lived in Linkinhorne, and his father was the Rector there. I think that Glyn helped Liz with the heraldry plaques. Strangely enough his girlfriend, Tamsin, phoned me out of the blue a couple of years later and asked me to meet her in Truro. I was curious and decided to go and what she wanted was my advice on whether she should marry Glyn or not. It was very strange as I didn't really know either of them that well, but I asked her how she felt about him and whether she could live without him and still be happy. If the answer was " no " then she should marry him, if it was yes, she should think very carefully and ask herself why she was marrying him. I couldn't help her any more than that. Very strange to get me involved in her decision, but I didn't follow the outcome.

***

At first things went relatively smoothly. I juggled dealing with 'Ideas in Design' and Debenhams, but there, Hillary offered a lot of help as she was with the Truro shop and 'Whirligig'. After Malcolm left she threw herself into work and seemed to enjoy taking on all the responsibility. She still left me little notes in the shop, saying she was always there for me should I change my mind, but I prioritized Jan. Earning enough money to deal with the losses caused by the high interest rates and the ever increasing problems from Debenhams, kept my mind active, and I was moderately successful in the brokerage business, any money from the small margins I faithfully split with Chris and paid into the bank with the details he had given me, but it would be a long haul unless something big broke to do really well. The conversion on enquiries and sales was probably less than 10% so it was a lot of work for the small returns. I was working at home in the evening on everything which pleased neither me nor Jan. Then suddenly everything changed. Chris and Liz had been touring the U.S. bases in Germany in their caravan. Apparently one night Chris had gone out and Liz was left alone in the caravan. She went to light the calor gas stove when it exploded; she swallowed a huge ball of fire killing her instantly. Chris came back to find everything ablaze. This is what he told me in a phone conversation.

***

After seeing to Liz's funeral, which he organised from Germany, he went on to join Liz's sister Carola who lived in Florence. He decided he was not going to live in England anymore, but was going to live with Carola, in Florence, just coming back to sell the house. Apparently he had fallen out with Liz's father and brother, and was closing the brokerage business in the U.K. as he wanted no connection over here. He said that if there was anything I wanted from the house I could take it, as he had no interest in what was there, and everything was going to be auctioned off. He added that there were some children's toys that I may be interested in. I went over with

Jan and apart from the toys, Jan fell in love with a little china flower ornament, although it was chipped, we took it back with us. A month later Chris turned up with Carola to sell the house and he came to visit me and explain that I was welcome to carry on if I wanted to with any of the contacts he had given me but I was not to deal in oil, silver or gold as he was going to run that business from Italy, but anything else I was involved in did not concern him. He was in a very jolly mood and I was surprised at how close and affectionate he and Carola were, considering it was only two months after Liz had died. I wondered if something had been going on between them before, while Liz was still alive. Carola was younger and more attractive than Liz and the reaction between the two of them was definitely as if they were a couple. Anyway, Chris wanted to know whether I had taken his 'Cape de Monte' china as he could not find it anywhere. I produced the flower ornament that Jan had liked and asked if that was it. He said it was one of the pieces and did we have the others. I told him that was the only piece I had seen. Then he noticed the chip on it and said that it was very valuable and I had damaged it. I told him that it was already chipped when we saw it, and then he flew into an uncontrollable rage, swearing and 'effing and blinding' and calling me a liar. I never saw him like that before. I remained calm and told him he was frightening Jan and the children, and asked him to leave. He glared at me for a moment, and then looked as if he was going to hit me. Carola was looking apologetic and coaxed him away; she kept mouthing "I'm sorry" to me. Eventually I got him out of the door and closed it behind him. I never saw or heard from him again. He was a strange man and seeing him in that light, I wondered whether Liz's death really was accidental. It certainly seemed convenient for him, and I could see no sign of grieving.

CHAPTER 16

A MILLIONAIRE AT LAST?

It was shortly after that incident when I received a phone call, first from Elliott in Florida and then another from Bill in Abu Dhabi asking me if I would like to join a chain of brokers trying to put together a huge loan from Saudi Arabia to a large American institution. It was highly secret and the loan if it materialized had to go through a very circuitous route, as it was imperative that the lender did not know who the borrower was or from which country until the deal was completed. Bill asked if I had a broker's license and when I said I didn't he said that I should contact a guy called Terry Mitchell who would put me in touch with a broker who wasn't too greedy and could be trusted, I could work with him comfortably he said. When I phoned Terry Mitchell he introduced me to Ron Wadham a mortgage broker in Launceston who lived in Bude. Terry said that he would work under my instruction. As the deal began to take shape the sheer size of it was staggering.

***

We had to organise a chain of fiduciary banks from the Saudi Bank in Jeddah to the Bank of Monaco to Credit Suisse in Geneva to Saltzburger Bank in Munich to Coutts in London and finally ending up in a small bank in America called Elkhart Bank. Various brokers were involved, in Jeddah and in the Gulf, in Germany, in Paris, Ron Wadham and myself in Cornwall, in Florida, in Los Angeles and in New York, so eight brokers and five bankers all looking to earn from what turned out to be one of the largest private money transactions. My job was mainly liaising with the fiduciary banks in London and Monaco, although I also dealt at times with Switzerland and the other agents Elliott, Jim, Betty and Bill. As one of the main links, I was privy to what we were trying to achieve and it was staggering, it was nothing less than a loan of $10 billion from Saudi Arabia to a large institution

I cannot name for legal reasons situated in the United States. I still have the text of the final agreed terms sent to the Bank of Monaco for onward transmission.
***

On successful completion a total of 0.5% commission was to be shared equally among all parties involved. Although Ron Wadham and I were considered as one unit calling ourselves Cornwall Associates, it still meant if we pulled it off Ron Wadham and I would share $3,846,154. Despite the telex machine with the frenetic activity surrounding setting up the chain etc., I soon ran up a horrendous telephone bill of over £3,000 and when I couldn't pay it my telephone was cut off just when matters were coming to a conclusion, but I still had the telex machine. I sent a telex through to all my contacts telling them that because of the time difference they should telex me to notify me that they were going to call me. This would give me time to get to the office where I could take their call, as my home line was faulty. I then gave them the telephone number of the telephone box in the car park down by the beach. Dealing with Paris, Monaco, Switzerland and Abu Dhabi was alright provided nobody was using the telephone when I got there as those calls were during the day. The trouble came with calls from Elliott and Jim who would call up in the middle of the night. The telex machine would start up at 2 or 3 0'clock in the morning and the bell would ring in the house. I would then have to jump out of bed, throw some clothes on, run down to the car and drive down to the beach to await the phone call. Once when I got there, a man was already in the phone box about to make a call. It was about 2.15 a.m. when suddenly he jumped as the phone rang. He picked it up and then turned and saw me waiting outside the box. He opened the door and asked me if I was expecting a call from Los Angeles, it was Jim on the line. I thanked him as if everything was quite normal, told him I wouldn't be long and took over the phone box. I could still see the surprise on his face as I left.
***

Gradually against all the odds and through all the suspicion and subterfuge the deal started to look as if it might be serious. Ron Wadham invited the family to tea at his house in Bude. He was extremely excited to be involved in such a powerful project. For him it was the first time he had strayed outside his little world of mortgage lending and to be honest he had to do very little except give Cornwall Associates the credibility of a finance broker's license. I dealt with all the negotiations keeping him informed as we went along, and I am not sure that he grasped the complexities of what we were trying to do. Ron Wadham was a tall spare man in his late forties, very conventional and straight laced. He lived in a pleasant house the other side of the Bude Canal and kept goats in his long garden. His wife was a very pleasant lady considerably younger than him and I believe that it was his second wife who also had been his secretary. I understand that he had two children by his first wife, and they lived with her. We spent a pleasant day there, it was bright and sunny and we had tea on the lawn. The boys enjoyed playing with the goats and Jan seemed to get on well with his wife. Ron kept saying to me that he couldn't believe it and did I really think that the deal would come off. I tried my hardest to play it down, telling him that there were still many probable pitfalls ahead, and not to raise his hopes, but try as I might I couldn't dampen his excitement. His wife couldn't believe how blasé Jan was about it all, she was as excited as Ron and was busy telling Jan all the things they wanted to do with the money, but Jan said that she would be very surprised if it was successful, as there usually was something that went wrong at the last minute. Then it finally looked as if everything was in place and the loan was actually going through. I had to send the following telex to the Bank of Monaco for onward transmission to Jeddah:-

"Text of Telex to be sent to Prince………. in Riyadh as discussed:

"We refer to discussions that have taken place with regard to the provision of a sum of 10 billion

U.S.Dollars on the following terms namely: Term 15 years: Emission 96: Interest 10.25 and understand that there is a substantial Western government entity whose identity may not be disclosed formally at the present time but, from informal information given to us would be acceptable. We require a formal application and request for funds in terms already advised and on receipt of the same will respond immediately with a view to bringing the matter to an early closing and will also advise modus operandi. Please indicate on which day you would be able and willing to close this transaction?

Signed For and on behalf of the Bank of Monaco."
***

The money was to pass from Jeddah to Monaco, to Munich, to Geneva, to London, and to Elkhart in U.S.A. From that point on it was out of our hands. The American brokers were to gather at the Holiday Inn in Elkhart, and the European brokers at Claridges in London on the day of signing. Betty had booked a suite at Claridge's; Ron Wadham and I were invited along with Joel and Bill who was flying in from the Gulf. It was November 1979. We all gathered together on the appointed day in Betty's suite, drinks and sandwiches were sent up while we waited with apprehension. The phone was constantly ringing, and some gentleman who was Betty's assistant, was answering it in one of the other rooms and relaying the information back. Then at 11 p.m. our time, it happened, the papers were signed and the loan transfer was to be put in motion. Everyone in the room went wild, Ron Wadham and Joel were jumping up and down on the bed like a couple of children and Betty and Bill were hugging each other and her assistant was sitting on the floor weeping with joy. To be honest they were all pretty drunk, as it had been a long wait and the nerves had kept the drink flowing. Everyone was going crazy, except me. I sat in the corner by myself unnoticed, not really believing what had happened, it was still very unreal to me. Then Ron Wadham and

Joel shouted across wanting to know why I wasn't celebrating with the rest. I said that I would save my celebration for when the money came through. Apparently Betty had booked us into rooms at the Dorchester for the night, and as it was after midnight I thought I would take advantage of my room and go to bed. As we went to depart, there was a call from Elliott in the Holiday Inn at Elkhart. He sounded equally as excited as everyone else and he had phoned to say that he had spoken to Steve and Steve had said that it could take anything up to three months for everything to be finally put to bed.

***

When I got back I told Jan what had happened, but like me she said that she would believe it when it was actually finalised. A couple of days later I had a telex from Elliott asking me to put in my formal application for the commission due to Cornwall Associates. As I typed out the invoice to be lodged with the Elkhart Bank for $3,846,154. 00 it suddenly dawned on me what getting that some of money would actually mean. My share would be $1,923,077..00, more than enough to fund the Debenhams project with a hefty surplus left over, and Ron Wadham had suggested that I should invest in property, as that was what he was going to do. I talked it over with Jan and she said that, if it really was going to happen, perhaps we should start looking at buying a large family property where there would be enough space to lose her mum and dad. Then I saw it advertised in the 'West Briton', the house of my dreams. It was in Mawnan Smith, and was castellated looking more like a castle, with gardens running down to the Helford Passage and its own private beach. I phoned the agents and got the brochure sent to me. It was beautiful and in such an idyllic setting and all for a mere £795,000 and the agent said that they could well accept an offer of probably around £700,000. It was empty so Jan and I went to see it, and it was all we could have ever dreamt of, with huge rooms, each showing the most wonderful views from each, and it had a completely self-contained wing, which had been the staff quarters, perfect for Jan's mum and dad. If we really were going to be rich, all the other agents were already celebrating and sorting out their investments, then this was the house for us. But caution still registered and I would do nothing until the money was in my account.

***

I realized I had put all my eggs in one basket and staked everything on this coming off, as 'Ideas in Design' through the high interest rates of 20% on its overdraft was hemorrhaging money at an alarming rate. The Debenhams business was booming and we were carrying anything between £75,000 & £100,000 over a one month period costing us nearly £2,000 a month in interest alone and now the bank were cutting back and insisting that we could not exceed £50,000 which meant either long delays on orders or we were going to have to start turning business away. A crisis was looming which only this commission could solve, and despite everyone telling me that my troubles were behind me and that I was rich, I still found it hard to believe. I had been close before and I remembered the crane business with American Hoist & Derrick which would have solved an earlier crisis.

***

As usual for me in my life, more care problems were mounting. The first slight setback occurred when the automatic gearbox on the motor caravan packed up just as I was about to leave for Exeter, Taunton and Bristol to check on our business after the January sales. Then the head of one of those slippery snakes started to appear, and it was going to be a long one. Firstly Debenhams wrote to me asking me for my proposals for opening up in the remaining stores. I telexed Elliott to ask how things were progressing with our commissions, and he telexed back to say that they had been trying to get in touch with me. They had been phoning my office number, but he was sure that the phone was being diverted as although they had left several messages with the different people who eventually answered, each time, they had also got some very funny replies. I shuddered to think who had been answering the phone down by the beach. He added that there was a crisis and he needed to speak to me urgently. I rushed up to the house and asked Jan's mum if I could take the call on her phone, very reluctantly she agreed. I then went down to the telex machine and sent him through the number, getting back up to the house just as the telephone was ringing. The news was the worse I could have expected. The large American Institution, having received the money, refused to recognise the brokers involved. The American brokers had threatened to sue and basically the borrowing institution had said the equivalent of "See you in court", confident in the knowledge that it could take forever and be extremely costly. But apparently the brokers were determined. They had formed a legal entity with the sole purpose of pursuing the matter to the end, and getting everything that was due to them plus costs. Each member had to put $20,000 into the kitty to set the ball rolling and so far ten of them had joined in. The agent in Jeddah and the bank in London had opted out. London, because it was beneath them, and out of the bank's charter to get involved, and the Jeddah agent, because he was probably double dipping and had already received a fat pay-out from the Saudi's, he couldn't risk that getting known. That just left me; they always seemed to ignore Ron Wadham. I told him I was broke and the response was "Well Ronnie if you're not in, then I'm afraid you'll get nothing, we can't carry passengers. Think about it - $20,000 for over $3 million. You've got seven days to come up with it." But I was in such a mess I knew it would be hopeless. I wandered down to the phone box with a pocket full of coins to phone Ron Wadham and break the news to him. I honestly believed I could hear him crying in the stunned silence on the other end of the phone. Then with a sob in his voice he said, even if he could raise the $20,000 it wouldn't stop there. The large American Institution with all their money could keep the case going for years racking up the costs. The dream had ended - he would just go back to his normal brokering. At least it hadn't cost him anything he said... No it hadn't, I was the one lumbered with the costs and now I had no telephone, and a business that was being drowned by interest rates, not to mention, I was behind several months on the repayments on my Audi.

Chapter 17

THE DREAM TURNED INTO A NIGHTMARE

The Snakes won't leave me alone! There came two more blows. The first came when interest base rates hit 20% which meant the bank was charging me 24% and that meant that my entire working margin was consumed by interest rates, there was nothing left to pay the staff and I had no reserves to back it up. The second, was a letter from Dennis Angilley, virtually quadrupling our rent on the Truro shop when our lease came to an end in August.

***

Yes, the snakes had risen and were out to get me this time! With regards to Debenhams, I decided that I would go to see them and I would drive up in the Audi and plead my case. I stopped off at Taunton services station for refreshment, and when I came out to the car park, there were two men standing by the Audi. Lucky for them and the worse possible news for me, it was pure chance, they were going down to St. Agnes to **repossess** the Audi, and like me, they had stopped off at Taunton Services for something to eat and drink, and they just happened to see the Audi. They had all the paperwork and they demanded that I hand over the key. I couldn't argue, all that I could do was ask if they could drop me off at the station so I could catch a train, which they did.

***

At Debenhams I asked if they could give me an immediate release of the money they collected from my counter, or at least a weekly payment, failing that I would have to terminate the contract. They told me that they could make no exceptions in their procedures as it could lead to all sorts of demands to vary contractual terms, and they then reminded me that I was bound in a legal contract that would only come up for review at the end of the year, until that time I was legally obliged to continue. All my arguments fell on deaf ears and I left having achieved nothing and minus a car. I had to get the train and bus home and was not looking forward to explaining things to Jan. As for the business, under the circumstances I could only delay or trim the payments to the suppliers and I knew that would eventually blacklist me and dry up all my sources of supply. Maybe, I could just keep the ball in play until the end of the year at the cost of sacrificing my business and then with the bank loans and guarantees I needed to find another source of income.

CHAPTER 18

NOW TO RE-INVENT MYSELF

Now I needed to find a job to support a wife and four children. So I got the local paper and scanned situations vacant, but I realized I really wasn't qualified for anything advertised. The only job with a reasonable salary that didn't immediately appear to need any qualifications, was as a manager of an estate agency with 'John Julian's', so I applied for the position. Obviously, I had never been an estate agent before, but I certainly had Management skills. 'John Julian', being a large department store, with an estate agency attached, almost met my concept of a property shop. Then there was my stint as an interior designer, which made me familiar with property. So as usual, when I needed information in a hurry, I went to the local library and brush up on my knowledge of the estate agency business, and the history and background of 'John Julian'. I did all this, and felt pretty confident, added to all that, my friend Keith Turner, gave me a glowing reference, as I had used him as a sponsor; as he was a mortgage broker I thought that it might help my standing. Anyway, armed with all this superficial knowledge and Keith's help, I managed to talk my way into the job, much to my surprise and relief. Unfortunately, it was also to the surprise of all the existing staff there, as Clive Burge, a qualified surveyor, and assistant to the previous manager, had been expecting to take over as manager by all concerned.
***
I didn't experience until later the animosity I would find. At first, before I could join them as the new manager, I had to spend a month at the Newquay estates office to learn the ropes, and I to go through my probation period. I kept a low profile and got on well with the manager and staff, there, taking their orders and doing what I was told. It was the end of a hot summer and I couldn't help but find it incongruous to be standing there in my suit talking to some

bikini clad holiday maker and her husband who was wearing brief swimming trunks. They had seen a property in the window and came in to talk about it and I had to take them off in the car for a viewing, I definitely felt overdressed. On at least a couple of occasions the enquiries came from very shapely woman in brief bikinis, and one of those shapely women, I had to take by her to show her round an empty flat. I felt particularly uncomfortable; she wanted to view the property by herself. It was like following this woman from room to room in her underclothes and trying to assume it was normal.
***

I was enjoying the work though, and one property I had to take a prospect to, was quite spectacular. It was set almost at the bottom of a cliff with a steep drive leading down to it and seemed to be set on a carved out rock platform. It was in the style of a Roman villa with a lot of marble and columns; the swimming pool was surrounded by classical statues. However, it had been empty for a long time and there was a sad air of decay about it. It was rapidly decomposing into a classical ruin. Had, I the money, I would have snapped it up, but the restoration needed vision and this was sadly lacking in the potential buyers I took to see it. When I left Newquay it was still unsold and had attracted no serious interest.
***

After my training, and when I eventually got to the Falmouth office, I could feel the hostility from the staff there as I arrived to take up my new position which they all clearly felt should have not been offered to me. Sensing the atmosphere, I called the staff into my office and asked what the matter was. There was Clive, and other staff in the estate agency comprised of Mary Long, an elderly lady who really ran everything, and a young girl junior called Cassandra. There was also the staff in the department store, who also resented my appointment but I reckoned I could deal with them later. Mary was the sort of person who would never beat about the bush, and she gave it to me straight. Clive had set his heart on the job and was more than qualified to do it, and I had come in from nowhere, they knew nothing about me, but clearly Clive's experience of working there far exceeded where-ever I came from. In a way I was grateful to her for laying it on the line to me because I now knew what bothered them all. I totally agreed and said that I could empathize with them why they thought my appointment was outrageous. Yes, of course Clive should have been given the job and not me, the management must have strangely over-looked his value to them and it did not seem to make sense from what they confided in me, I could see why that would hurt, and annoy the staff. But they gave me the job, and I needed the work. I went on to explain that I was in a bad financial position and couldn't walk away from it, however much I agreed with them. Perhaps we could come to some compromise. I thought that it would be only fair if I shared the managership with Clive. From henceforth, we would share everything together and we would consult on every decision to be made and I would certainly do my best secure a raise for him in the near future. This seemed to pacify them all and I made sure that I dealt with Clive with due respect. It also helped me, as knowing nothing about the job, I could learn from Clive as we went along without him noticing.

***

As it happened, we became great friends and he was of considerable help to me, not only at 'John Julian's' but also with the various things I got involved in later. With harmony in the office, the department store staff accepted me too, and I got on well with them all. I learnt that my predecessor had suffered from drink and depression and had died of a heart attack. Through neglect, the agency was now scrapping the bottom of the barrel. It only had four really saleable properties and scarcely a dozen all told on its books. In a bid to attract more properties, I slashed the sales commission to 1.5%, half what the agents were getting. That meant of course, I was then immediately ostracized by them, I had walked into a cartel. However, it had the desired affect and soon Clive and I were working overtime in taking on properties. This was also bolstered by extending my catchment area. There were no other 'John Julian 'agencies west of us, so I considered anywhere to our west fair game. My stay at 'John Julian' was to prove very interesting. Maybe, if I could just reach for the Ladder later.

***

After putting 'More Snakes than Ladders' together the author still needed to search for solace in his life. He decided to take a round the world trip calling on friends and visiting countries with intrigue. With a clearer head upon his return in early 2014 he intends to release the 3^d edition of 'More Snakes than Ladders' in which he goes into detail about his tragedy and how he needed to re-invent his life.

Marc and Giles-Trisha's twins

Adam and Simon-Craze

Old boys' reunion

Grateful dead house/San Francisco

Troy as a punk

Jan and I got married

Nick Sand photographed by police after his St Louis laboratory was found in 1973

OPPOSITE: John Griggs with

Nick Sands & Tim Scully

My sister Trisha as an airline stewardess

Parents outside St. Albans house in Herts

Mike Druce

Keith Turner & Avril

Jan

My first visa picture

Setting up shop

Charles Schoenfeld & wife

Printed in Great Britain
by Amazon.co.uk, Ltd.,
Marston Gate.